# 27 Letters

## P.S. God Loves You

Angie Marie

# Dedication

This book is dedicated, first, to my firstborn, Madison Suzanne, whose artistry and determination inspire me every day.

My gentle momma, Suzanne Rachel, who loves me best.

My daughter in heaven, Callie Grace.

My darling youngest child, Marissa Kate, who loves with a pure heart.

My granny, Bernadine, who loved with the love of Christ.

My delightful sister, Terri, who came home on a most memorable December day wrapped in pink (after three brothers) and who was my live baby doll. You will always be my little sis.

My aunties, all who have shaped my life by pouring love into me.

My friend Anna, whose grace overflows. And to her precious daughter Gracie, who is a true miracle.

My friend Marcia, who was my second mom and Madison's birthday twin. Those eleven birthday collaborations here on earth were pure joy.

My exuberant teaching mentor, Lucy.

My gals at the coffee shop on the boulevard—Rachelle, Christina, Ellen, Katy, and Liz—for good coffee and good cheer.

My husband, Kevin, and my big brother, Steve (aka Uncle Hoss), who each have me by the hand as we walk through many full circles together, both in obedience and in awe of the Lord's leading.

# Contents

# Foreword

For as long as I can remember, I have seen Angie as the most amazing person I've had the pleasure to know! I have been blessed enough to know her my entire life, being her baby sister. She embodies the role of nurturer and exudes love and kindness, spreading joy wherever she goes. I knew when her children were born that they would be the most fortunate children in the world.

Angie's words come alive in this memoir. One can truly feel the love she has for her firstborn daughter, the recipient of these beautiful, eloquent letters. They are so God-inspired and Spirit-filled, it's nearly impossible to put them down! Each letter demonstrates the unfolding of a beautiful journey confirmed by visions, dreams, and words, all of which create a full circle of healing, forgiveness, and pure love. These letters are written to her daughter, but their content applies to you and me in our daily lives. She has inspired me to rise up, to pay more attention to how God is speaking, to ask Him to show me more through my dreams, and to record in writing His impressions on my heart. These well-organized pages are a blessing—to the original recipient, to me, and to anyone who has the honor of reading them.

It's a heart thing!

Terri M.

# Preface

This self-assigned writing project originated from an idea to write letters to my oldest daughter for forty consecutive days leading up to both her golden birthday and her move abroad. The letters intersect with a memoir style of journaling that has been unfolding in tandem with my spiritual healing and awakening. While writing to my daughter, God impressed upon my heart to share my stewardship of His tender mercies with a wider audience. I don't claim to be an expert on any of the subjects contained in this book. The architecture of the letters is my own journalistic creation of how I process thoughts, emotions, and revelations. It is my intention to share what I've gleaned as a traveler down life's roads from a storytelling perspective. This is a compilation of 27 letters given to my daughter on her 27th birthday. I pray my words will bless you too.

# Introduction

I invite you into a private world where I write, pray, and seek counsel from heaven. It is my great hope that you will be inspired to tell your stories in your own unique way. I encourage you to write to those you love, to write for the sake of writing. As you do, I pray you will grow closer to God as He uses the Holy Spirit to remind you of who you are to Him. His glory is unfolding in this world like never before. May His love fill you to overflowing.

# Cover Letter

## Farewell, For Now

Be still, and know that I am God;
I will be exalted among the nations,
I will be exalted in the earth.
(Psalm 46:10 NIV)

**June 11, 2022**

Darling and Dearest Maddie,

We miss you already; that is certain. I've always known you would venture far away from home. I will stay focused on how proud I am of you and count the days until your return(s) home. I will not be sad, because this is such a grand opportunity for you.

In the years to come, you will speak often of your time in Sweden with no remembrance of the days you longed for home and your people. You will be changed forever in all the best ways.

I started this letter project for you on April 1, 2022. I wrote for forty consecutive days, intending to create 27 Golden Birthday Letters for you to read while you're away. Read them in order when you feel led to do so.

The project did not unfold at all as I had planned, which I mention in one (or more) of the letters. The letters are essentially a snapshot of my daily journaling with you on my mind.

Before I started writing regularly, a year ago or so, I didn't have a framework for the concepts I share. The frame around my writing is unfolding in real time, with increasing clarity as I press in to share what has always been on my heart.

I hope my words will bless you in ways you maybe didn't even know you needed to be blessed. I followed the Spirit and pushed through some roadblocks along the way. Writing is like that, especially when emotions are involved. Life is like that as well.

Every. Day. I will be here praying for you and cheering you on. And I am with you in spirit, always.

Go get 'em!

I love you so very much, Precious Daughter!

XoXo,

Mom

# Thoughts from Home Whilst You're Away

Never forget who you are, never forget
where you came from and why you are
here on this beautiful planet.
—Euginia Herlihy

**April 1, 2022**

Twenty-two years ago today, when you were just four years old, we moved into our 800-square-foot 1936 fixer-upper, a.k.a. The Little Brown Bungalow by the Bay. You cried off and on for weeks, saying, "I just want to go home." Yes, me too, honey; the introvert in me usually just wants to go home.

But look at you now with your grand sense of adventure and mighty determination to live this life so fully, to see the big wide world out there.

No matter how far away you are, I know you will always keep home in your heart. I foresee your introverted homebody spirit coming back home to "rest" as you begin settling into the future family

God has for you. I know you will return with great inspiration toward your destiny. I speak forth the family God showed me in your future.

Isaiah 55:11 says, So shall my word be that goes out from my mouth; it shall not return to me empty, but it shall accomplish that which I purpose, and shall succeed in the thing for which I sent it.

On that note, the words we use, especially those of our prayers—because we partner with God—shape our lives. You know this, honey.

Manifesting (the world's version of obtaining desires) from the spirit world is a real concept that really works. Therefore, we must speak Jesus over our prayers, our petitions, our decrees, and our declarations. Then, what we cultivate will be a part of a larger divine plan that can only bring blessing and protection to our lives. The counterfeit versions of manifesting our dreams and desires will never yield fruit long-term.

What is in your heart—those great big dreams—is only from one source and can only be truly and satisfactorily fulfilled from that source, which you know is the true living God.

We either tap into light or darkness; there is no in-between. I want to say this here as well: We are in an epic spiritual battle on a global scale. In so many ways, it is being paralleled in our own individual lives.

I want to emphasize that it is not a political battle, though it is being waged in that arena. Nor is it about Republican versus Democrat.

Perhaps I personally have communicated in a manner that makes it seem so. If so, please forgive me.

The battle is presently playing out like a bad movie, often under the guise of conflated social issues propped up with false dichotomies and evil schemes yet to be fully revealed. That is the war that, exceedingly ironically, President Biden described as "a fight for the soul of a nation." Indeed. And I do believe he and those who puppeteer him are on the wrong side of history.

This ain't your granny's religion or politics of which I speak. And yet I taught you girls to refrain from political or religious discussions. I meant to protect you from the gaslighting aspect of said discussions, which often result in the loudest person shutting down any dissent—the most "tolerant," of course, carrying the biggest sticks and loudest megaphones.

As for Granny's religion, my granny/your great-granny was a perfect example of God's love. (I knew nothing of her politics.) I have cultivated her spirit of love and taken over her mantle as prayer warrior for this family. She spoke no words of judgment over anyone; she spoke only love and encouragement. I realize now, years later, that she was truly filled with peace because she fully trusted Jesus. She lived so simply and authentically true to her core beliefs. Perhaps more about Granny later.

As for choosing judgment over love and true teaching, the Bible, in 1 Corinthians 13, says that the law without love is as loud clanging cymbals. I'm sorry for the cymbals that clanged in your spirit through our family's collective experiences with religiosity where others tried to enforce their own version of the law. Though I do know you recognize there were, within specific settings, beautiful demonstrations of God's love. God has used those years, all of them, to plant good seeds in your heart. I choose to be grateful to the characters in that part of your story because they were all your teachers—even while some of them were ironically effective non-examples, operating from a place of religiosity, and therefore condemnation.

I know it has been a challenging task of holding on to God's truths while disentangling from the damaging thought constructs, which haven't come from the Father's heart for you.

You know quite well that many in organized religious communities are ruled by a religious spirit. Perhaps unknowingly, they seek ultimately to control, coerce, or otherwise manipulate others under the guise of religious convictions. That is why the delivery often comes with shame, blame, and guilt, all of which are cheap substitutes for building genuine relationship. It is the quality of the relationship that inspires others to be their best, and not just in a classroom setting, but in all relationships.

Matthew 7:16 (NKVJ) says, "You will know them by their fruits." (That is a good test.)

As I close today, I speak healing over the ways in which you've been hurt by religiosity, even if indirectly or within our own family, some of whom God has shown me to be quite full of false moral authority. There are those who self-righteously bust people over the head with a God Stick even as they bear little fruit in their own lives.

But the fruit of the Spirit is love, joy, peace, forbearance, kindness, goodness, faithfulness, gentleness and self-control. Against such things there is no law.
(Galatians 5:22–23 NIV)

I forgive them—all false moral authorities who have hurt me and/or those I love. We are called to love them anyway. The forgiveness journey was not easy for me; it was a spiritual root canal without anesthetic, but it has brought great peace to my spirit. I am undergoing quite a restoration, which I hope is evidenced in what I am sharing from my heart.

For today, I break off all damaging effects of the religious or political spirit (twin maladies) over you, and Marissa too. I ask God to use those experiences that wounded you and turned you *away* instead of *toward* Him as a continual guide in your life and as a powerful testimony for others who have also been similarly hurt. They need your grace and your love and your wisdom. The best we can do with our pain is to forgive fully so we become helpers to others who haven't yet found redemptive healing and wholeness.

You may not realize it, but you are already guiding and steering others toward their God-given destiny. You are gifted with thoughtful leadership, self-discipline, and a mighty sense of determination. That is a testimony in and of itself. You also possess many gifts of the Spirit.

Cheers again, my beautiful daughter, to your grand adventure in Sweden. It's inadequate to say how proud I am of you. I am truly, and have always been, in awe of your spirit, your might, your intelligence, your creativity, your stunning beauty, and your endless talents.

I am blessed to be your mom. I want to be more like you.

I love you, honey. To the ends of the earth and beyond, I love you. I'm here praying, always. Today I just felt to pray away any dusty old remnants to make room for the new. I speak God's complete refreshment over you.

*You are my heart.*
*XOXO, Mom*

(I covered a lot of concepts in this first letter as one thought unraveled into the next. Stay with me, please, as a bigger picture will unfold.)

# A Bit More about God Sticks, Religious Spirits, and Heaven's Authority

The treasures of the heart
are the most valuable of all.
—Nichiren

**April 2, 2022**

Oh hej Sweetie (see what I did there?),

I was cruising down the boulevard on my way to the coffee shop one day when I heard this familiar verse in a real way and felt it deeply in my spirit. "That at the name of Jesus every knee should bow, of *things* in heaven, and *things* in earth, and *things* under the earth (Philippians 2:10 KJV). I thought, "Where did that come from?" I wasn't thinking on these things. I've since had many more experiences of this sense of quickening to things of the Spirit.

I felt God revealing to me personally, though many others are speaking of it, that a revival is coming in order for many more to know Him. It was impressed upon me not to worry if the world seems to be falling apart. He said not to be afraid; He is pouring out on His people in greater ways. There will be increasing signs of divine wonders and miracles. Everyone will hear the gospel and make a choice. There will be no more fence riders and no more high horses (religious, political, or otherwise).

About a year later, on the same drive down the boulevard, I had a similar impression in my spirit telling me, "The Bible is coming to life, and the Word will dance off the pages; the seemingly far-fetched stories will become modern and true to life." I believe the time is here, and with greater increase, we will begin to witness that which can only be explained as God.

Since then, the most common Bible verses I've heard many times, in almost a cliché manner, have danced off the page in banners, flowing like ribbons across the sky. As the words press into my spirit, I hear them fresh, new, and so real. I am only beginning to understand why the Bible is called the living Word.

Because of my mom and my grandma, I have always felt a reverence for God, but you know I did not grow up with Bible verses being any regular part of the speech in our home. I knew all the cuss words though.

As covered in yesterday's letter, through misguided teachings as well as our family's collective experience with those afflicted with a religious spirit, I learned more about what it's like to be hurt by a religious spirit than what it's like to feel God's love through others.

How often lies about who we are and who God is come from the very places we should be learning about God's true character and experiencing genuine demonstrations of His love.

God Sticks, as aforementioned, are simply tools of religious-spirited, misguided persons who either believe they are doing right or seeking, ultimately, to fulfill a selfish agenda. The misuse of God's Word in this way has spoken lies about God's true character and how much He loves us. It is a wretched Guilt and Shame Gospel, which does not reflect the heart of God. Though our negative experiences did not happen within a specific church congregation, we know this "gospel" sends many away from churches. Sadly, this is how the enemy has marched in the back door of many people's lives.

I believe the time has come for a healing redemption of those who have been hurt by religious institutions and/or religious people. Churchy people who carry the anti-Christ spirit of religion are going to be either redeemed or removed. Because they have stood in the way of God's love for His people. They have modeled the antithesis of God's heart for us.

I see a lady wagging her finger at me when I ran into her at the dentist office, telling me she hadn't seen us at church in a long time and I really "*should* talk to God once in a while."

I kindly smiled and said, "I don't need to go to church to talk to God." I felt a revolt in my spirit against a feeling of judgment, though I know she meant well, and I knew her to be a kind person.

But doesn't that personify what so many people reject about church, religion, and so-called Christians who seem focused on counting other people's sins? It was a poignant moment in my understanding of what I was running from. Perhaps that was the moment when, as my mom would say, "I'd had it (religiosity, that is) up to my eyeballs," and maybe because what I wanted to hear was that we were missed.

Your generation often says, "I am not religious, but I'm very spiritual." This can mean a lot of things, but I take it to mean that you've rejected church/organized religion but still seek the spiritual. Unfortunately, this often amounts more to new age practices than actual relationship with Jesus. This is another way the enemy has come into many people's back door. The front is bolted tight; the back door is wide open.

I believe we are in an awakening of great magnitude. Millennials, and all generations, will begin to understand how prevalent and intentional the spiritual misguiding has been.

The spirit world of psychics and energy healers and such, though they are often kind people who truly desire to help others, is not heaven's authority. Though indeed spiritual, it is often not God, even if it seems good. Heaven's true authority is a revelation from the Spirit of the Lord Jesus Christ. The spirit world is a serious place, and we must know what/who we are tapping into.

How, then, does one dial up the Lord? Simply pray to Him and ask Him to speak to you, to show you things. And then listen to that still small voice, which for me is most often a spontaneous flow of words impressed upon my spirit. Sometimes I get dreams, visions, or repetitive signs such as number patterns. It helps tremendously to write down what you hear/perceive, as it invites God to confirm His words to you.

There are only three sources you will hear from: God, the enemy (accuser), yourself.

> Call to Me, and I will answer you, and show you great and
> unsearchable things, which you do not know.
> (Jeremiah 33:3 NKJV)

Even if what I share has little credibility now, I know it will make all the sense soon enough.

May it give you thoughts to ponder, and may you pause to reconsider the ways in which your generation has been filled to overflowing, by design, to make room for little else. There is often a self-centered focus on spiritual matters and/or social issues where (literal) signs preach a collective good but there is no real problem-solving. I know you perceive this great irony as well as the hypocrisy of preaching tolerance while spewing vicious and even violent rejection of any speck of dissent. This particular spirit, akin to a religious one, can be strongly felt in the city of Seattle.

May you understand *more* of the spiritual awakening that the world, including your momma, is going through, and may the seeds of the Living God be watered in you today.

God has shown me *you* as a worship leader again. I declare this to be part of your destiny and your life's purpose in Him. I have precious memories of you at age five or so belting out "Our God Is an Awesome God" while riding in our midnight-blue Isuzu Trooper. You were a joyful child, always fully trusting in God's love for you and always, always singing a melodious tune. I love you for that (and so much more).

Did you know your singing brings me some of the greatest JOY I've ever known?

I pray you'll learn some worship songs and sing them to us at Christmastime when you get home. Swedish songs will do as well. I'm so looking forward to Christmas 2022! I'm decorating a new tree this year with all vintage ornaments I've been in the process of collecting. I wonder if Sweden is a good place to search for vintage treasures.

The best treasures, of course, are those you carry in your heart. It's always a heart thing.

My heart is happy because you're my daughter.

You are my greatest treasure.

I love you, Madz!

So much,
Momma

# Feet Dreams

When you wash a person's feet, you find
out why they limp like they do.
—Bill Johnson

## April 3, 2022

I had a dream the other night about calloused feet. I thought of your athletically calloused feet. Since God has been speaking to me in dreams and visions, I seek to understand the message therein.

The dreams I've been having are different than even the vivid dreams I've had most of my life. Segments of dream episodes are highlighted by the Holy Spirit as I pray into the deeper message. As I am transcribing my dreams into my journal, I often receive an interpretative message in my spirit. I believe there is deeper meaning still; I expect further revelation will come, as will more complex heavenly dreams.

I hope to learn much more about biblical dream interpretation, but for now I am trusting in God to highlight what is of importance.

This dream about feet came the night after Dad and I waited in line for over an hour to go into an estate sale in Seattle. It was cold and windy; my feet got so cold, they went numb. I stood in line studying everyone's shoes as I tucked my frozen nose down into my coat collar.

In the dream, I was standing with a person I have not understood over the years. I easily connect with most people and find that, even when I feel socially anxious, I can talk with anyone. In this person's presence, however, I struggle to find a connection point and then begin to feel anxious. It seems we both feel awkward. I have wondered what her experience in my presence feels like. Since you went to school with her daughter, I have had many encounters with her. Sometimes I've felt annoyed at some of her comments, which seemed strange, out of place, or even unkind. But I know we simply don't understand one another.

In the dream, we both took off our shoes, as we had returned from an event together that involved a lot of walking. Our feet were similarly covered in callouses and sore spots, but in different locations on the foot. Seems like a pizza dream at this point, right? But, as with many of my dreams of late, I could not dismiss the dream from my thoughts throughout the following day.

Late in the day, this interpretation spontaneously "dropped" while I was not consciously thinking about the dream:

Unless you have seen someone's feet (not literally), you do not know the path they've walked, and you do not know their sore spots/wounds. Do not judge them for the shoes they wear (again not literally), which cover their wounds and sorrows of the world. They may be more like you than you can ascertain, and they may even appear to be having an easy road to travel, but they have traveled a wilderness road too. Love them. Consider that their feet hurt as much as yours do at times.

The next day, in search of vintage Christmas ornaments, Dad and I went to another estate sale. While standing in line next to some kind strangers, we talked for fifteen minutes or so before entry, mostly about estate sale experiences. One gal pointed out the other gal's espadrilles, which were pineapple themed. She told the story of how she purchased the pineapple shoes as part of a costume and wasn't sure, she said, why she'd worn them that day.

How did more shoes/feet become the focus of the conversation? Perhaps it seems insignificant and random, but it is clear to me now how God speaks to us in repetition until we understand His message.

At the day's end, I "randomly" chose a sermon by a pastor I just recently started listening to. Nearly every sentence of his sermons is a take-home biscuit. He ended his sermon on forgiveness with the quote at this letter's opening.

To add to the synergy, I had spent the previous forty days writing about forgiveness. The Lord gave me a writing assignment, *The Forgiveness Tour*. He took me through quite a wilderness walk. He told me the writings would become a book. I ended the tour with a culminating project, stamped with an urgent due date—a one-day notice—to write a letter of forgiveness to a person who hurt me deeply: your father. I'll share that letter with you soon because it represents such breakthrough in all our lives.

And so it is, I set down all my pain, sorrow, and bitter, bitter roots at the *feet* of Jesus. And He, in His incredibly synergistic ways through the Holy Spirit, has spoken such confirmations to my heart about the journey we are on.

I walk forward from here on in others' shoes, whether they fit me or not, whether they are covered in pineapples, which may have significant meaning of its own, or whether my own feet are sore.

I recently felt led to buy Terri a cool pair of shoes for her new journey as a 207-pounds-lighter version of herself. I later realized the significance of the timing and that the shoes have peace signs sort of hidden within the swirly design. Much to her delight, Terri discovered the incorporated peace-sign design on the third wearing of the shoes. In fact, there are peace signs within the color swirls, but there are also iridescent peace signs that can only be seen in the sun.

We are the peacemakers, those of us who walk with others.

We are all, indeed, "just walking each other home," as the quote by Ram Dass says.

Journey on, sweet girl. You have and will continue to forge many paths that others have not the courage to walk. Walk into your dreams and your full destiny. And take as many others with you as you can.

I love you so much.
Your momma bear

P.S. While pineapples are never directly mentioned in the Bible, they've been used as a Christian symbol to represent, among other things, friendship.

# On the Power of Words

## A Little Bit about a Lot More That Remains to Be Said

The words we speak become the house
we live in.
—Hafiz


**April 4, 2022**

Darling Daughter of Mine,

I should share with you, as I may do in a cover letter, that I am writing these letters to give to you just before you leave for Sweden in early June. I hope they will provide comfort from home, a little momma love, maybe even a take-home biscuit when you need it.

I also feel I am on assignment to write forty-day projects toward a bigger plan God has for my life. Perhaps the assignments are the *stuff* of my books. And by *stuff*, I mean *content*. And by *stuff*, I also mean *stuffed* because I've had multiple dreams now of books stuffed with thick pages that look like those bakery cellophane window boxes. Instead of pastries or donuts, the boxes in my books are filled with the mementos and the clutter of life. (I took the dreams, partly, as a sign to make decluttering revisions of my volumes of writing, a task on which I have yet to embark.)

We are blessed that we can FaceTime and text one another while you're away (hopefully); that will make the miles and oceans between us seem less vast. Nonetheless, there is something so special about the written, even if typed, word. I hope you will write back whenever you can, even if we are able to speak often.

Feel free to journal any thoughtful replies in one notebook that you can wrap up for my Christmas gift when you return home in December. Eek! I'm already so excited for your homecoming! Though I don't wish to fast-forward you through your amazing adventure of working in Sweden and traveling Europe, I will count the days, every single one, until you come home.

My thoughts have been dwelling so much in the written word, the spoken word, and the power of our tongues. It's another one of those concepts few of us were directly taught either at home, school, or church, all of which should have been instructing us on how much our words shape our lives. This would be my main do-over as a parent (i.e., the power of words and how to utilize it well).

Many of us, especially those who grew up in forms of neglect, abuse, or chaos, at some point begin to speak word curses over ourselves, as we take over for those who spewed insufficient, untrue, or even cruel words toward us. We internalize the negative words, and we make them true. We also, ironically, dismiss the power of words themselves because they—good or bad—can become tools of manipulation for bullies/abusers and other impure-agenda-driven people. We learn to tune words out as they lose their meaning; in doing so, words become more casual than they ought.

> If I speak in the tongues of men or of angels, but do not have love, I am only a resounding gong or a clanging cymbal.
>
> (1 Corinthians 13:1 NIV)

When referring to my growing up with a verbally, and sometimes physically, violent stepdad, I often spoke of a fat/ugly/stupid tape that ran a loop in my head. It sounded humorous to others when I would call it such, but it wasn't a joke. I would always get a laugh when I summarized my teen years as fat/ugly/stupid. Perhaps the best uncomfortable reply was a nervous courtesy laugh. I don't speak those words over myself anymore. I've long since forgiven my stepdad, who has both apologized and repented for his abuse. Forgiveness makes room for immense gratitude. The Montana ranch life he provided is one of my greatest blessings. But isn't it such a lie that words don't hurt like sticks and stones?

Additionally, we are prone to fill in the blanks when we don't get necessary verbal feedback, often drawing wrong conclusions about ourselves and others. The truth is, if a person who has a significant role in our lives cannot provide us with encouragement and honest, constructive feedback, our relationship with them will limit us. And sometimes the absence of words, albeit instructive in itself, is as painful as the presence.

On that note, I ask you to take your every thought and word captive. I know this is an area of personal work you've been doing for some time; I know you are finding victory in doing so.

Consume truth, revelation, light, and goodness that feel like sunshine to your soul. Turn that into healing words; let them spill out of you everywhere you go.

I pray today you'll recognize all word curses in your life, that the Holy Spirit will reveal them to you so that you can break them off your soul. I pray you will speak healing, redemptive words over yourself and others, which will bring more life and love and blessing.

For this letter, I'll end with a prayer for you:

Lord Jesus,

I pray that Maddie, my beautiful daughter, will declare every day, by the power of her tongue, that which she deeply desires in her heart. Those deep desires in her heart are Your dreams planted there toward her destiny. May she speak key Scriptures over herself that will yield the peace and the joy and the other fruits of Your Spirit in her. I break off all word curses and lies anyone has tried to speak over her or the enemy has tried to plant in her head. I cover her thoughts and her words in the redeeming power of Jesus. I speak blessing, favor, and protection over her. Lord, as always, keep her safe in her coming, her going, and her staying in. Bless her indeed. And let her bless others with her powerful words. Amen.

How many oceans are between us? It matters not because in our hearts there is no distance.

I miss you so much though.
Momma

# Wherein I Share a Dog Dream
# and a Lengthy Impartation

The Lord is my shepherd, I lack nothing.

> He makes me lie down in green pastures,

he leads me beside quiet waters,

> he refreshes my soul.

He guides me along the right paths

> for his name's sake.

(Psalm 23:1–3 NIV)

## April 5, 2022

I would like to share Dog Dream two of three I had in recent months. Below is my journal entry from the following day:

I dreamed about a German Shepherd again last night. It seemed to be a different dog than in the other German Shepherd dream, a little lighter in color.

The dog belonged to the Hatloes and came right to me as I walked into their home to visit with Jennifer. There were multiple dogs present, all over the living room, but it was the German Shepherd that came to me. It nearly laid itself on me, resting its head on my shoulder, as I sat down on their couch. I tensed up even as I started petting it. Jennifer asked me if I was okay with the dog hanging on me, and I said, "Yes, I love dogs, but I'm a little scared it may bite me." I asked her if the dog could feel my tension and would react badly as a result. She said to massage its shoulder area and it would be most content, which forced me to wrap my arms around the dog and fully embrace it.

I asked in my prayer time the following morning, Am I afraid to give myself over to the Lord completely? Am I still afraid to trust anyone? I'm not sure, Lord, so I am asking You to speak to me now.

I first typed out my own advice (a great way to step into God's wisdom). Everyone can hear the voice of God. He wants to speak to all of us with impressions upon our hearts, but we must get quiet long enough to listen. Center yourself, and start writing what He downloads in you as soon as you ask Him to come. He is not late: He is always on time. And He is a ready friend, always there when you speak His name.

Here is a portion of what the Holy Spirit poured out:

You are holding back because you've been hurt and you do not know if abuse and trauma can be healed, even by Jesus.

Keep calling on My name and keep receiving/giving grace. It's okay to hold back as you redraw boundary lines, but I want you to know you are safe now. I won't allow the hurt or the abuse any longer. You've endured enough, and I promise you, though it seems like wasted years and pointless arguments, I am using the evil for your good. It has been evil behavior. You are not wrong to call it such. Evil only comes from an enemy, and all of it came from the enemy.

Until others surrender fully to My voice and stop serving their own will, they cannot change. This is not for you to determine or to sort out or to facilitate. But you will know. I tell you I am continuing to break down the strongholds that have been a part of your life. Let Me work, and always pray for others.

I am revealing more and more truths, and I am also bringing justice. You are Mine; you are precious; and you did not deserve even one day of the abuse, the sorrow, the pain. My light shines on darkness, and My light has come. Arise and shine! The generational sins of pride, arrogance, selfishness, and spiritual abuse are the strongholds I am defeating.

I sent the German Shepherd again to remind you that I am here to comfort you and that you can rest in Me. Do not fear. Enjoy the comfort, the soothing calm, of My presence. I am your Shepherd, and I am with you always—even when you're frustrated and want to spew the ugliness back at those who've harmed you. The dog represents the comfort of My presence, and the more you relax into that, the more you surrender, the more peace and calm you will have. It will be like sitting in the presence of a protector and a loyal, true friend all at once, no matter what is happening around you, and no matter what others do/don't do.

And then an encouraging bit about writing.

I want you to stay on this track. Keep writing every day, and I will turn your diligence and obedience into something you cannot yet imagine. Even when it comes together as a finished product, you will feel awed at what we have created together. You will be in disbelief of your own creations because you haven't believed in yourself, and you have worried about the criticism of others. I will keep the critics quiet. I will make loud the voices of confirmation and affirmation because this good thing you do in sharing your heart is truly for My kingdom.

You say, "But Lord, I'm only one voice, and why me?" And I say, "Why not you?" This is how I am taking your suffering, that which the enemy meant for evil and that which the enemy tried to rob from your life, and using it all, not just for your greater good but for a larger picture of kingdom purposes.

Do not analyze which elements are present in your writing; you do not need to cover all the right spiritual bases to write a legitimate guide that will help others. I want you to write it as you are doing, as a guide for those who feel unqualified to write their own stories. Let them know that all they must do is follow Me, listen to Me, and take the action of writing down what they are hearing. Tell them, your readers, to write it down even if it seems from their own head or an echo of some past voice of condemnation or even a ringing of something they want to be true but aren't certain it is. Writing is excavating, and it is the recording of you hearing My voice. It is an impartation of My wisdom into your life. Keep digging this ground, even when it feels dry and cracked and impenetrable, especially when! There is treasure to be excavated, and the harder you work, the greater the treasure. And yet the work will often come easily because you are partnering with Me.

Do not get frustrated and move away from what I am calling you to do in this time. When you feel weary, come to Me, and I will refresh you with My living water. You have done well to push past, right through, write through, the clogs. Use poetry-style writing when you're stuck, just little words and phrases that pack a punch, expressing intense feelings that feel complicated to explain. Readers will identify with the essence of the message and do not need, or even want, in-depth explanations where you've often felt the need to overexplain.

You've felt this need because what has happened to you in your life seems almost unbelievable, and you feel you must present enough facts and explanations to convince others. This has been a trick of the enemy.

No, you do not need to prove anything. I am your counsel, your only counsel. Speak the pain out and declare your victory. Then your breakthroughs will keep coming to you. I want to use the pain to help you help others. This peek inside your heart is the way. Keep writing, keep writing, keep writing! I will reward your every minute, your every word.

Put your full trust in Me to help you create something meaningful and beautiful. Even those who know you well will learn about you, things they thought they knew and things they didn't know at all. I am telling you that your readers will pick up your book and read it cover to cover without putting it down. They will be compelled by your humble, honest approach; they will feel your honor and appreciation for them.

This is your time to let people into your world. You have felt different your whole life, feeling as if you live a private existence inside your head, which no one understands. That is quite true. But bring it out of you now, keeping the introspective wisdom I've designed into your being but also sharing what is good and beautiful. Hearts will be moved. Hearts will be touched. Hearts will be healed—your heart included.

That was a whopper of a download. Perhaps the very word *download* feels unfamiliar to you. It's a new concept in my life as well. I can't stop the pouring out now, and I wouldn't want to.

You may need some time to absorb the process that God is taking Dad and me through, individually as well as collectively. It's all good!

May He—the Holy Spirit—pour out great, path-guiding revelations in your life as well. When He does, you will know it's not your own clever brain talking or the enemy spewing more lies. You will feel it deep in your spirit.

I wish you revelatory impartations that light your soul on fire.

Thank you for opening your mind and heart to what I desire to share with you, my firstborn and most lovely girl.

I love you.

God loves you.

XoXo,

Mom

# A Dog Dream Wherein God Introduces a German Shepherd

The Lord is your protector;
The Lord is your shade on your right hand.
The sun will not beat down on you by day,
Nor the moon by night.
The Lord will protect you from all evil;
He will keep your soul.
(Psalm 121:5–7 NASB)

## April 6, 2022

The following is the first of three Dog Dreams I had several months back; it is the first dream I have ever recognized as being from God:

I was at a large event, maybe a class reunion. Many people were at the venue, which seemed to be a community center. I could only discern one distinct person from my past, my classmate Bridgette, though I knew everyone in the crowd. She was a loyal friend from high school who truly cared about me. As I was walking around the event, a German Shepherd kept following me. I felt afraid he was going to bite me, so I tucked my hands up into my long sleeves. The dog continued to follow me, either trying to nip at my hand through my sleeve or put his paw up to my hand. I asked my friend Bridgette, "Why is this dog following me everywhere? Is he going to bite me?" She replied, "No, he just wants to be your friend; he keeps trying to hold your hand and walk with you."

I usually forget my dreams before I finish my cup of coffee, but I could not stop thinking about the dream. There is weightiness to things from the Lord. I asked in prayer, "Lord, are You speaking something to me through this dream?" I seemed to get no answer.

Later in the day, I had an appointment at the Apple Store. As I was waiting in queue, a woman with a German Shepherd walked in and sat literally right next to me. Her dog plopped down and went to sleep nearly at my feet. I said (under my mask/under my breath), "Lord, is this the dog from my dream?" Down in my spirit, He spoke: "Yes, this is the exact dog from your dream; enjoy my sense of humor in confirming the dream was from Me."

I pondered the dream's meaning for days but resisted fabricating an obvious or corny tale. I'm new at this process.

In a spontaneous download a few days later, I heard this:

Lay down your weapons, take My hand, and walk your wilderness journey with Me. I am Your Shepherd, a friend who sticks closer than a brother. Take My hand as I showed you in the dream of the German Shepherd. I am your loyal, faithful companion through My Holy Spirit. You must do these things: lay down your worldly weapons of protection, and take My hand. I surround you and protect you and your family in all things. Someday, you will know all that I have sent My angels to do for you.

Further research on the biblical meaning of German Shepherd dog dreams, though I'm no dream interpreter (yet), confirmed my download and should be put in the context of the spiritual wilderness I've been in to reconcile and redeem the locust years of my life where I walked with a firm grip on my worldly weapons of warfare. I note that worldly weapons of warfare, while they can feel like a plausible means of protection against pain, ultimately invite pain to stay. Some of my weapons included cynicism, denial, unhealthy independence, anger, self-condemnation, and the like.

Sweetie, may you lay down your weapons, whether they be critical attitudes, self-deprecation, comparisons, rationalizations, justifications, or any other barriers that focus you on looking down rather than up. Look out and look up. God is waiting for you to wait on Him. When you do, your life will be an anticipatory, single-minded focus on what God is doing in and around you. You will see Him in everything; everything will be prophetic. Don't miss the many ways He talks to you.

Take His hand and let Him lead you through. Wait upon Him. At all times, wait upon Him. Your life will be a continuous flow of answered prayers as you wait upon the Lord. An Old Testament meaning of *wait* is to "whirl in the dance." (I heard this wonderful concept in an online sermon by Bill Johnson.) And so it is; we pray with a happy expectancy as we wait on God.

> But they that wait upon the Lord shall renew their strength; they shall mount up with wings as eagles; they shall run, and not be weary; and they shall walk, and not faint.
> (Isaiah 40:31 KJV)

I speak answered prayers and divine appointments over you each and every day while you're in Sweden and forevermore.

Whirl in the dance, sweetheart! Joy will always come when you do. His promises are Yes and Amen.

Golly, I love you!
Ma

# A Little Prayer for You This Day

Whoever dwells in the shelter of the Most High
will rest in the shadow of the Almighty.
(Psalm 91:1 NIV)

## April 7, 2022

Dear Jesus,

I ask that Your praise will ever be on Maddie's lips, that she shall be fully healed, restored, and delivered in all the ways You know she needs to be. Make the words of her testimony a blessing to her generation. I stand in faith for things unseen, and I know that You are carefully constructing everything for her good. You are there with her now through every struggle, doubt, and fear. You are with her in her joy as well. I give her, my precious child, over to You again this day. I call on the Holy Spirit to speak to her heart now. I pray also that the gifts of the Spirit come in full measure to her and through her. May others feel You when she speaks, when she smiles, when she laughs. She is an encourager!

I cover Maddie this day and every day in Your precious blood and ask that You hide her always in the shadow of Your secret place, that every measure of protection goes before her, behind her, and beside her. Let her not be afraid of what is happening in the world. The world waits on pins and needles for Your mighty hand to move now. They will see that You are a mighty God whose hand can only explain what is evidenced in front of their own eyes. This is a restoration project that is being paralleled in all our lives. Restore, refresh, and renew us even as You restore our land.

Thank You, Lord, for ever-so-gently bringing Maddie back to You. Thank You for all the restoration projects in this beautiful earth You've created for us.

Amen.

*Love you so much, honey. You are His.*

*Momma*

# Dog Dream No. 3

## A Large and Personified Black Dog

But the Helper, the Holy Spirit, whom the Father will
send in My name, He will teach you all things, and bring
to your remembrance all things that I said to you.
(John 14:26 NKJV)

### April 7, 2022

Why am I sharing my Dog Dreams with you? Because I believe they
are from the Holy Spirit. As previously shared, when I ask the Lord
in prayer what they mean, I usually don't get an immediate answer,
and then, often when I'm going about my chores, pondering mostly
random thoughts, I will have a sudden download. I quickly dictate
into my phone's Notes app or write down the paragraph or so that
comes within just a few seconds. It's been an interesting process that
I pray will continue to unfold in greater ways.

Another Dog Dream:

I don't know the dog's name. It was a large, very strong black dog. It had decided it was not going to obey commands. I was remarking to you girls as I was trying to get this dog to cooperate that it had gotten out of control. You were making us one of your beautiful charcuterie boards when the dog started reading expirations on packages of crackers. Like a human, the dog was "pointing" to the expiration date, in an almost antagonistic sort of way, telling us the crackers were expired. I told you girls how very smart this dog was. Even as I climbed up (Up!) a ladder that happened to be positioned under a light fixture (The Light!), the dog stood up on its hind legs and attempted to reach me. It wasn't able to hurt me, but I was fearful, as I felt I could not get away from this dog, even if I climbed higher. It was a very commanding and muscular dog. I tried to shout commands, but the dog kept jumping up toward me and challenging my authority.

During my prayer time, the following verse was highlighted for me the very morning after I had this particular Dog Dream:

> Behold, I give unto you power to tread on serpents and scorpions, and over all the power of the enemy: and nothing shall by any means hurt you.
> (Luke 10:19 KJV)

I believe the dog represented the enemy, someone who seemed friendly enough but who was challenging my authority over it/him. Then it was trying to trick me into thinking it was more than a dog so I would soften my stance and relinquish my authority. Wow.

I also believe it was a warning of the enemy's schemes and tricks coming from someone/something once believed to be friendly and/ or someone who deceives others. It was an illustration of power from a being, per se, who—like the enemy—has no real authority. I am therefore warned to take my authority in Christ against all enemies so God will not allow them to harm me.

I pray this over you today, Sweetie, my best charcuterie board maker:

May you tread on serpents through the authority you have in Christ Jesus to command all darkness to flee from you. I cover you and your home and your vehicle and your person in the precious blood of Jesus, that you may be protected by the hosts of heaven and hidden in the shadow, always, of the secret place of our Lord Most High.

Amen.

My prayers may sound religious to you at this point; I'm okay with that, as I'm learning how to pray, how to command, and how to use the spiritual authority we are given as children of God. I take my authority, and I am making serious inroads through all the darkness that was once a part of my life. I've already sent the hosts of heaven to guide your path and all the details of your time in Europe. God has gone before you, and He will be with you in all things. You are hidden in His safety. I declare and decree this today.

Psalm 91 (NIV):

> Whoever dwells in the shelter of the Most High
>> will rest in the shadow of the Almighty.
>
> I will say of the Lord, "He is my refuge and my fortress,
>> my God, in whom I trust."
>
> Surely he will save you
>> from the fowler's snare
>>
>> and from the deadly pestilence.
>
> He will cover you with his feathers,
>> and under his wings you will find refuge;
>>
>> his faithfulness will be your shield and rampart.
>
> You will not fear the terror of night,
>> nor the arrow that flies by day,
>
> nor the pestilence that stalks in the darkness,
>> nor the plague that destroys at midday.
>
> A thousand may fall at your side,
>> ten thousand at your right hand,
>>
>> but it will not come near you.
>
> You will only observe with your eyes
>> and see the punishment of the wicked.

If you say, "The Lord is my refuge,"
   and you make the Most High your dwelling,
no harm will overtake you;
   no disaster will come near your tent.
For he will command his angels concerning you
   to guard you in all your ways;
they will lift you up in their hands,
   so that you will not strike your foot against a stone.
You will tread on the lion and the cobra;
   you will trample the great lion and the serpent.

"Because he loves me," says the Lord, "I will rescue him;
   I will protect him, for he acknowledges my name.
He will call on me, and I will answer him;
   I will be with him in trouble,
   I will deliver him and honor him.
With long life I will satisfy him
   and show him my salvation."


Aren't the psalms beautiful?

I previously didn't appreciate the Bible enough because I didn't understand it, but I knew I was supposed to. At the Assembly of God church in Granite Falls, MN, where my mom and my granny took us to Sunday school, we used to sing, "Read your Bible, pray every day, and you'll grow, grow, grow." I thought it might make me taller, but that was the extent of my understanding. In later years, hit with the aforementioned proverbial God Stick, I thought that if

I didn't read my Bible and pray every day, something bad was going to happen to me or to someone I loved. This idea was aided by the enemy, who used my dad's suicide to condemn me, starting at age three, into thinking his death was somehow partly my fault. That's a story for another day.

For today, I admonish you to stand up in your God-given authority. The devil has power, but he does not have authority, so you are always above him. Keep him always under your feet by speaking these words when needed: "Rise up, Lord, rise up in me; enemies, get under my feet and back to the pit from where you came."

As a follow-up note, for the next couple of nights after this dream, a black dog crossed our path some distance in front of us as Dad and I were out for our evening walk. The dog had its tail tucked and seemed to be walking away in shame as it looked back at us. The second night, we saw the dog at another point on our route, but just for a fleeting moment, and it disappeared into the night.

This game of connect-the-dots is getting more interesting by the day.

I have confirmations in the natural of what is transpiring in the spiritual. God is truly amazing me!

Stay tuned!

Rise up (in your God-given authority)!

All my love,
Your momma

# Divine Dog Dreams

## More Revelation from
## a Morning Writing Session

My sheep hear My voice,
and I know them, and they follow Me.
(John 10:27 NKJV)

## April 8, 2022

I will be your friend and your protector as I showed you in the dream of the German Shepherd. Think shepherd. You are one of My sheep, and you hear My voice. You are not his sheep, and you aren't one of the sheeple in today's cancel culture of virtue signalers and false unity. Stay strong and stand firm! Because even those who are doubting you, pushing back, are watching you closely. They are pushing back because they are in rebellion and because they are terrified that you might be right. You are right about the rightful president. I have given to My prophets the truth of what I have called forth in your nation.

Be informed, and be calm and pray on how you will gently speak My truths when others come to you and ask you how you knew. Teach them how you learned to hear My voice and how they can surrender their hearts to Me. Your gentle love will bring them into My gentle love.

Keep stepping in as you do every day; your obedience and hunger are being rewarded. Keep writing long past the forty days. I want you to fast one full day before you edit your forty-day stretch of writing. Let Me guide you in wisdom, discernment, clarity.

I will show you what you need to know.


Have you found it an interesting connection that you have been gifted dog-themed pajamas for many Christmases or that you have a small collection of dog-themed housewares? Perhaps that's a stretch. But as I look around, I see dog décor even in our home (things collected before it was trendy).

Is it true that *nothing is a coincidence*?

The answers don't really matter because the more you see God, the more you see God. And that can only be a good thing.

May you see Him today, in everything, and in every thing.

Woof! Woof!

I love you, and I hope joy is evidenced even in the serious notes of my letters to you.

My heart leaps when I see your joy.

Love you so much,
Mom

# Heaven Come Down

And my God shall supply all your need according
to His riches in glory by Christ Jesus.
(Philippians 4:19 NKJV)

## April 9, 2022

Dear Maddie,

I am speaking God's divine destiny over you today. I declare that
you will awaken to this great truth: we are made to carry His glory.
He is our Creator, so what else could be our higher purpose on this
earth?

What is His glory if not His great favor? In the glory is all healing,
truth, life, peace, lasting joy.

Understanding God's glory is a very new concept for me. I press
in toward a deeper understanding with each new day.

Something I've been feeling viscerally as of late is a thinning of
the veil between heaven and earth. It's as if heaven is coming down
to meet us. How "right there" is the spirit world at all times. And
that world knows no secrets. There are dark forces always waiting to
hijack our prayers and our words, that they may never reach as high

as heaven. I send the hosts of heaven to cover you and your prayers today and every day.

Heaven come down and pour out on my daughter. Show her, Holy Spirit, how to access Your authority, Your healing power, and Your glorious riches. I break all false authority off her spirit and any ties with darkness or new age processes that she may not have understood as such. I bind Your truth to her soul. Amen.

The "enlightened" ideas of counterfeit authority/power have been packaged just for your generation such that they are seen as an evolution of an old, crusty religion that must be discarded like moldy bread.

The snag is, these practices bypass God and may work for a while but eventually return void, or worse yet, they invite darkness.

As it says in the Bible, God is the same yesterday, today, and forever. He never gets moldy or stale. We, if we don't refresh our spirits in Him, are the ones who grow stale.

There is much I've learned about new age culture. The title itself suggests something fresh and new. I appreciate how far out, how too religious or reminiscent of a truly stale version of religion, this may sound to you, honey. It's okay; I meant to remind you that Pete and Repeat went out in a boat. Pete fell out, and who was left? (Don't worry, Pete was wearing a life vest.)

I know you will know in time how things are not at all what they seem. You surely must conclude, since you know me to not be a person afflicted with a religious spirit, that divine revelations are truly unfolding.

We are in the midst of the Third Great Awakening as many are proclaiming. Revival fires are spreading to a location near you. My own spirit is on fire.

I want to share a prophecy I received on March 1, 2022. God speaks to me in many ways now that I know how to listen. (I'll tell you even more later about the structure I've created for inviting this process and how it is unfolding in my life.)

This day, I felt the Holy Spirit come over me with a broader message to the body of Christ. I was in the shower when I received the following energized message, which felt in my spirit like urgent marching orders:

Awake! Arise! It's March, and it's time to march! My ecclesia, march, march, march! My eyes are on you, the eyes of March. The earth and everything in it is Mine. Four-leaf clovers (Matthew, Mark, Luke, John), three-leaf clovers (the Trinity), fields of green, rainbows of My glory and My promises shall fill the earth. Pots of gold filled with heavenly and earthly riches shall pour out on My people. Every symbol and logo created by the Lord your God is being taken back into its true meaning.

And then a message to me specifically:

I give you the key to unlock the doors to My glory and riches. You are coming Full Circle. Give grace everywhere you go, and look for the fives. And in your writing: protect ~~the guilty~~ the forgiven. You are through the wilderness now, in pastures of green, as promised in My Word.

Mile marker five was highlighted for me later in the day as I drove past a gas station I've driven by for over twenty years but had not previously seen the marker. Biblically speaking, five equals grace, goodness, favor. (It's also my birth date, I must point out.)

There is the element of engaging our brain's reticular activating system (RAS) that helps us see what we'd like to see, but as you read on, you will realize God often uses numbers to talk to people. Perhaps it's Him engaging the RAS that He designed into our intricate brains.

I'll share more about the March 1 download tomorrow, as it kept coming throughout the day. As time "marches" on, I know that what has been spoken will come to pass. God does not point something out to do nothing about it.

Let the glorious love of God fall on you today, lovely girl.

I love you to the moon,
Momma

# Wherein I Continue to Share What the Holy Spirit Speaks

He lets me rest in green meadows;

he leads me beside peaceful streams.

(Psalm 23:2 NLT)

## April 10, 2022

Another download portion from March 1, 2022:

It is March; the world is turning green. It's the green of pastures and meadows and My promises to bring you out of the wilderness and into your peace. [He gave me a vision about a year ago that I was walking through a dark forest. My instructions, again, were to lay down my weapons, take His hand, keep walking forward, and look up when I felt lost in the woods.]

You've been on a grueling journey, but you've been strong and tough as nails, sometimes too tough when you should cry and grieve—it is necessary—but I am bringing you out as a victor and not a victim. This is your Victory Story and the stuff your books are made of. You will find a day where you will be immensely grateful for all you've gone through, even the most painful tragedies, because they are becoming beautiful stories of victory that will bless so many. Your heart will be seen. And all will be vindicated in My truth. My rod and My staff, they guard you, they guide you, they comfort you. I have your daughters in My hands, and they are being brought out of a desert too. Great is My faithfulness to you and your home and family. Let Me. Rest now. It is done. Breathe. Create. All good things are yours, full measure, shaken together, pressed down, and running over.

I AM THE VINE.
YOU ARE THE BRANCHES.
MY BANNER OVER YOU IS LOVE.

LOVE HEALS ALL WOUNDS.
IT'S A HEART THING.

I pray that what I share about my journey back to our Creator will inspire your heart. I know this kind of "talk" can be offensive, so I share with vulnerable trepidation. (If you're still listening, kind thanks to you, honey.)

Even so, I feel pressed to share and more pressed to pray as I've done for many months:

Lord Jesus, draw my daughter Maddie gently back to You, that she may know Your peace, Your love, and the fullness of Your healing power. Bring her into alignment with her destiny, and call her to lead worship again as You've given me in visions of her future. Thank You, Lord, for Your calling on her life and for the fulfillment of her divine destiny. She is Yours, Lord, and I leave her in Your mighty hands of grace and love and every manner of protection. Surround her with angels, and continue to whisper into her soul how much she means to You, her Creator. Amen.

You mean so very much to so many.
We love you, Our Great Madino.

XoXo,

Momma

# Wherein I Decide to Write Approximately 1,000 Words about Melvin Oscar Anderson, Your Maternal Grandfather

Draw near to God, and he will draw near to you.
(James 4:8 ESV)

## April 11, 2022

April 9 was my dad's eightieth birthday. I don't know enough about him except that he was dearly loved by all who knew him, and I've missed him for nearly my whole life. Children were especially drawn to his deep, radiating kindness. He was troubled, tortured by unseen forces, but he loved others deeply.

A confusing lie told in some Christian circles is that all people who commit suicide go to hell. We may not know if they have given their heart to God, even in their last moments before death. I know my dad is waiting for us in heaven. This isn't something I tell myself to feel better about his absence in our lives. And I'm not debating (ever) theology; I find it difficult to accept that he would be further punished for his inexplicable pain. I believe God understands when a person sees no other way to end their suffering.

Here are a few facts about your grandfather:

He was one of five children born to Wilhelmina and Albin.

His paternal grandparents, Andrew and Augusta, migrated to Belview, Minnesota, from Malmöhus County, Sweden.

He loved to fish.

He loved Tennessee Ernie Ford.

He loved gospel music.

He loved to fish.

He adored his children.

He was highly intelligent.

He was artistic and creative.

He was a sharp student who couldn't settle in a school setting.

He loved to fish.

He was athletic.

He had a fascination with cars and got a new one whenever he could, however he could.

He had style.

He was James Dean cool.

He used alcohol to numb pain.

He is buried in Belview, Minnesota, next to his father and his brother Kenny (who died the following year in a bar shooting).

He was only twenty-six when he died.

His death was ruled a suicide, but it was more of an accidental self-inflicted gunshot wound, as my mom has explained in details I won't share here.

When you were the same age I was when I lost him (three years old), repressed memories began to surface. For over a year, I had nightmares about the night he died. Any sleep was synonymous with the nightmare. On repeat I had the dream, so I tried not to sleep, but nightly succumbed to an hour or so of terror before waking up terrified, turning on the TV, reading a book, having a snack: anything to get the scene out of my head.

I camped out in different rooms in the house trying to disrupt the nightmares. I was teaching full-time, so on such little rest, my mental health was thin. I had a wonderful class of third graders that year, whom I followed to fourth grade. We were like a family, and I'm certain they have no understanding of how God used their sweetness to bless me as I tried to be the best teacher for them during a difficult season of my life.

Though it seems obvious now, I did not realize the dream was the actual suicide incident or that it was even about my dad. It was like a festering wound in my soul, so deep and painful, I could not yet perceive it. Because it was a painful subject, any specific information about him and what happened to him had been withheld from me. Therefore, I made no connection to the specificity of the nightmare.

Here's the nightmare:

I was standing at the top of a staircase. There were many paramedics and red and blue emergency lights flashing everywhere. Someone was on the stairs covered in a white sheet. I did not know who was under the sheet, but I knew it was someone I loved very much. I did not know why they were under the sheet, but there was blood all over the stairwell. My mom was standing at the bottom of the staircase looking bewildered. Her expression frightened me. She didn't say so, but I had the distinct impression that I was not to advance down the stairs. I felt to advance down the stairs because I wanted to help. It was as if I could run to the person and love them back to life.

I would always wake up shaking, and sometimes crying, right when I made eye contact with my mom and her countenance became unrecognizable. I believe what I perceived in my mom's face was the shock and horror of what had happened. She was just twenty-one years old with baby number four on the way.

During the nightmare episodes, I began to have severe sciatic nerve pain. It became unbearable one early summer day as I was sitting in a teacher certification renewal class. I had to exit early due to the pain, as I could no longer sit. I thought it was recurring kidney issues, which had previously caused lower back pain. I was able to get an emergency appointment with my massage therapist. During the massage appointment, my dad's youngest brother left a message on my answering machine (pre–cell phone days). He called literally while I was in the massage session. We had never talked on the phone, so it was unusual for him to call.

I had seen some of the Anderson family at my Minnesota wedding, about twelve years earlier, which was our first encounter since my dad's death. We had been writing back and forth, my aunt Nona (Larry's wife) and my aunt Millie (my dad's sister), through the years since my wedding. But that day, Uncle Larry phoned me for the first time. He said he just felt compelled to call me. The message he left on our answering machine was "Hi Angie, it's your uncle Larry. I've been trying to get a hold of you all day. I just felt to call you and invite you to talk about your dad and ask me any questions you might have. I've been thinking of you and him all day."

I called my uncle Larry back that night. We talked, and we cried together for some time, simply amazed at the timing of what was simultaneously rising to our surfaces. We planned for me to visit him in Minnesota so we could spend time in person but also retrace together my dad's journey through his short life.

What happened next can only be divine appointments set decades in advance. I recognize that in greater ways as I retell this story now, almost another thirty years later.

Regarding the massage: I had a massage therapist who was very in tune to spiritual matters. She knew only that my dad had died when I was young. She said, "This is about your dad." It was as if she pressed a grief release button. The tears began to flow like a river. Oddly, I could not feel myself crying. It was such a deep well of distant tears coupled with a devastating feeling that my dad left us because I didn't love him enough and I didn't help him when he was hurting. The sciatic nerve pain left (and never returned) before the massage was over as the tears began to cleanse my soul.

Well, honey, wow, I didn't plan *any* of what I've been writing to you. I had some topics planned and haven't embarked on even one of those. Perhaps those will be another volume for another time.

With a growing impression, I perceive these letters to be a bigger assignment than what I set forth to do in writing you letters to open while in Europe. They are not much at all of what I thought I was going to share with you in writing. Whatever is unfolding, I pray it is blessing you, honey.

I love you, daughter of mine, granddaughter of Melvin Oscar and the lovely Suzanne Rachel.

He would have adored you so very much.

As we all do.

And thank you for listening. Did you know you're an amazing listener? You should give lessons on talking-less-listening-more because it is a rare skill you possess.

Bless you and your listening ears, which, interestingly, are the tiniest, cutest ears I've seen. You definitely got the ears in the family.

Big hugs!
the Lil Momma

P.S. I had a revelation about an etching of my dad's gravestone as I was printing this book for a beta reader. I share it in this postscript as follows: I framed the etching and hung it on our staircase wall right in the spot above where the person (my dad) under the sheet was lying in my dream. I had planned to create a full-wall eclectic photo gallery, but I never hung another frame on that wall for the next several years that we lived in that house. I realize now it was a grave marker of sorts that assisted me with my delayed grief.

# The Coroner and His Report

Call to Me and I will answer you, and I will tell you
great and mighty things, which you do not know.
(Jeremiah 33:3 NASB)

## April 12, 2022

My uncle Larry and I agreed on that June day in 1998, when we
spoke over the phone, to meet up in Minnesota later in the summer.
It was time for us to be reunited. We had some grieving to walk
through together. I didn't know at the time how my journey would
take so many others along whose grief had also been prolonged/post-
poned for the past thirty years.

Uncle Larry had many artifacts belonging to my dad. He gave me
family photos, my dad's lunch box and thermos, his fishing tackle
box, and a handmade knife used to fillet fish. He had a pottery-style
ashtray that my dad had made but felt to keep that, as he is very sen-
timental about his brother. He later gave the ashtray to Steve. I had
hoped for a sample of my dad's handwriting but was most pleased to
have some of his personal belongings.

Uncle Larry also had a copy of the coroner's report from my dad's death. The description in the report essentially describes some of the scene in my dream. Larry decided to call the coroner, whose name was listed on the report, though he was long since retired. He contacted said coroner, who invited us for an afternoon lemonade under the shade trees of his backyard. He said he'd retired many years earlier but still had the file for Melvin Oscar Anderson. He added that he remembered my mom and all the little kids left behind.

When we arrived, Dr. Opdahl had my dad's file in hand, which contained a love letter written to my mom. He asked me a few questions to assess my mental stability before giving me the letter. There it was: my dad's handwriting in a letter expressing his great love for us—his children, my mom, and our little family. Here's an excerpt from the letter: "You and the children are happiness to me. The five years I've known you have been the happiest of my life." -MOA

I'm not sure if the letter was gathered at our home or if it was still in my dad's possession at the time of his death. It was a time capsule preserved all those years for us. It was also a direct answer to my prayers.

Isn't it incredible how God goes before us? Even thirty years before, He gave Dr. Opdahl the inclination to file my dad's beautiful letter for the day I would stop by for a lemonade and collect my letter. It was a most memorable summer day in small-town Minnesota, going full circle back to my first years.

February 1, 1999

Dr. Opdahl,

This letter is long overdue, but I would like to express my appreciation on behalf of myself and my family for the documents you gave to us last August. We are grateful for the coroner's report, as it has answered some questions surrounding my father's death in August of 1968. The letter written by my father that was so safely tucked away in your file has been a source of comfort during our ongoing healing process. We thank you for your compassion in taking time to meet with us.

Sincerely,
Angie and family
Daughter of Melvin Oscar Anderson

We, Uncle Larry, Aunt Nona, and our little family (you, me, Dad, and sometimes Grandma), spent our time in Minnesota retracing some of my dad's steps. We drove, music blasting, windows down, to the places where my dad fished so many years before. We played Buddy Holly and other oldies that my dad loved so much. We cried together (I sobbed) as we let the wind blow through our hair and the delayed grief pour out of our souls. We drove to the church where the funeral was held and then out to the cemetery where I made the etching of his gravestone.

My mom was there for parts of the trip as well. She thanked me for excavating the past so she, too, could finish her grief. She talked openly about things she had not previously shared with anyone. Words to describe the beauty of reliving such tragedy in this way, with the people who needed to be there with me, escape me now and perhaps always will.

I'm having revelation, even as I write, that as we were speeding down dirt roads along the riverbanks of small-town Minnesota, singing along with "Rave On," we were capturing my dad's spirit, feeling his greatest joys, and capturing the freedom he must have felt when he was driving—too fast, windows down, dust trailing—on his way to his favorite fishing holes so many years before.

On the flight home from Minnesota, more of the impossible-to-contain tears poured out of me. It would be six more weeks before the faucet of grief, clogged for thirty years, would shut off. As I cried into my hands, trying to hide my face from others on the plane, you put your hand on mine and said, "Momma, I miss him too." In your little three-year-old spirit, you perceived precisely what was unfolding.

I'll leave you with a bit of simple poetry:

August '98

Thirty years have passed
Resting under a stone
With your father and your brother
Quiet peace
Life surrounds
Nature dances
My heart is still.

Amazing Grace

God forgives you
He understands pain
You didn't mean to take your life
He knows
You were searching
You didn't hear His voice
It's alright, Daddy
In heaven there is a place.

Rave On

When we all get to heaven
We'll roll back the rugs
Celebrate
Dance
Forevermore.

Go listen to some Buddy Holly tunes today or some Tennessee Ernie Ford. Your grandpa will surely join you in spirit. Oh, how he must delight when he hears you play guitar and sing! It would be his greatest joy on earth.

Sing sweetly and play softly a song for all that you have in your heart for him.

So much love for you, my sweet daughter.

Momma

P.S. I pause here to give a warm and grateful shoutout to my mom's second husband, who stood in so many gaps for our family as he whisked us off to Europe where we lived a happy little life that was sadly interrupted by divorce seven years later. I'm grateful for the reset button he provided by taking us on his military tours, far away from a particular chaos that needed more than a physical escape at the time. He loves me like a father should love his daughter. I treasure those stable, happy years of my childhood that happened because of my second dad. Our family is blessed to have him and Jeannie in our corner, cheering us on, celebrating our journeys, and thinking of us always. And how much richer are we that we are able to enjoy the beautiful Korean culture through Jeannie's delicious foods.

# Thought Life

## Casting Down Imaginations

For the weapons of our warfare are not carnal but mighty in God for pulling down strongholds, casting down arguments and every high thing that exalts itself against the knowledge of God, bringing every thought into captivity to the obedience of Christ.

(2 Corinthians 10:4–5 NKJV)

## April 13, 2022

The enemy brought much discouragement to me yesterday. With a migraine headache, I struggled through the thick pile of lies, including the one suggesting I should give up my writing assignments because they will bring humiliation to me and even embarrassment to my daughters. Among many lies, I heard, "You're too dumb to write." And this one too: "Your writing will expose you and open you up to criticism."

I take these thoughts captive, as they contradict what God has spoken. I know the enemy is threatened by our work, our calling, our assignments. Relative to the impact the fulfillment of our assignment has for God's kingdom is how powerful the warfare can be.

That tells me this: apply this idea to whatever you, Maddie, feel pressed in your spirit to pursue.

I must write.

It doesn't matter who writes more eloquently.

This is my story; only I can write it.

I do not write for the critics in the crowd.

I write for the person who grieves, who aches, who muddles through sorrow and deferred hopes.

I write for those who need to hear that victory belongs to those who use their words to call it in.

I write for the person who struggles to find adequate words for their pain, who feels alone in suffering but finds a bit of their own truth and redemption in mine.

I write for the person who thinks they can't tell their story. I write to give them permission to do so, to know everyone has a story that deserves to be written.

I write because I want to share more broadly the light of Jesus and His redemptive healing power in our lives.

I did not know, until I started regularly writing a year or so ago, that I—who had so vehemently rejected formal religion and religious people—would be writing about redemption or any other spiritual concepts. I'm more surprised than you.

I planned this set of letters to you to be a pleasant stroll down your Memory Lane, and mine as well, as I recalled the beauty of your childhood as seen by a mother who adores you.

I didn't plan to share the spiritual revelation and revolution unfolding in my life. Truth is unfolding all over the world. Everything we experience is being paralleled on a larger scale. It's a matter of whether we can see the "movie" playing out.

I pray my words won't feel self-indulgent to you, as I have let the Spirit lead me.

> So much SWIRLING in thoughts and ideas and arguments. The Lord is exposing us to chaos so we can truly understand PEACE. His peace is the absence of chaos.
> —Bill Johnson (emphasis mine)

Today, again, I pull down strongholds in your thought life too. They are lies about who you are.

I ask you to take them captive, then cast them out. Loose the lies from the layers of your soul, and bind God's truth (His Word), His love, and His peace to you.

Taking our thoughts captive essentially means that we challenge them until they come into alignment with the mind of Christ. Some thoughts will have to be run through many times. I hope I've demonstrated a bit of the process throughout my letters.

Use your strong mind to weaken the lies and rise up higher in the truths of who you are in God's eyes.

I love you, Beautiful Daughter So Dear.

Momma

# More on Feet, Shoes, and Walking

We're all going to the same place, and we're all on a path.
Sometimes our paths converge. Sometimes they separate,
and we can hardly see each other, much less hear each other.
But on the good days, we're walking on the same path, close
together, and we are all just walking each other home.
—Ram Dass

## April 14, 2022

I had another dream about shoes. In the dream, I was living
in a college dorm. The entry to each dorm room looked like the
old-fashioned glass storefronts. On display in the floor-to-ceiling bay
windows, on each side of each door, were shoes. A friend from high
school was living next door to me, and she had dozens of pairs of
designer Nikes displayed in her windows.

I admired in the dream, as I did in high school, that all her shoes
were adorable because her shoe size is 4.5. She and I once had the
same pair of shoes. I had seen them on-trend in Minnesota during
one of my summer nanny jobs there. I had to have them. They were

the typical white leather ASICS, called Tigers, with red and blue stripes. The shoe store in Rimrock Mall did not have my correct size, so I settled for a pair that were a size too large. They were a little sloppy and made me feel self-conscious. While I was wearing them, a mean boy at school who bullied girls asked me where I got such big feet. (He also told me I had fat chops and a big nose.) Between the mean comment and my friend joining the trend with her adorable size 4.5 version of the Tigers, I didn't wear mine much after that.

I've been seeing a homeless fella sitting on a concrete block across from my favorite coffee shop. I noticed a week or so ago that the sole of his tennis shoe was peeled back from the heel to the ball of his foot, almost completely separated from the shoe. I felt God tell me the man wears a size 12, to go buy him some new shoes, and to pray for him. In my spirit, I finally understood all the dreams about walking and feet and shoes: He is calling me to greater service, analogous to washing feet, a service that is about souls, not soles.

I didn't see the fella for the next few days, and then he was there again with a new pair of black ASICS Tigers(!) tennis shoes on. (Maybe I prayed them in.) Perhaps going and buying the shoes that day without question was where I was to step into obedience, but I was nervous and a bit unsure of what I was hearing, so I didn't follow through. I may have missed an opportunity to serve. I didn't miss the message, however.

Another week or so later, I saw him there picking angry scabs on his legs. Dad and I were together, so I had Dad give him some first aid items we had in the car, including salve and Band-Aids. We also bought him a latte and gave him some cash, for which he was most grateful. With slightly watery eyes, he looked up and softly said, "Thank you, and God bless you."

He must have moved his little camp because I haven't seen him since. I spoke the name of Jesus over him, as I do when I don't specifically know what to pray for someone, and as I will continue to do over every homeless person that I see. In our area, that is pretty near a full-time job these days. I don't know his story. I don't know how long he's been on the streets, though it appears many years. He may smell bad and look a bit scary, but he is precious to God. Is he just walking himself home all alone?

As you may have gleaned through these letters, one of the ways God has been speaking to me is through repetition and themes. If I hold myself to greater awareness, looking out and looking up, the alignment with the ways of God connects powerfully in my heart. Amazingly, the natural world directly connects to the spiritual.

He is pouring out His spirit in greater ways for all who are hungry. Many, even those who don't serve Him or know Him, will begin to have encounters. I agree with the proclamation of many others: this is a time of increase in signs, wonders, and miracles from heaven. I tell you again of God's hand at work in the earth so you can perceive with great clarity the times in which we are living.

My sister texted me yesterday about how she feels God pouring out on every aspect of her life. I shared my coffee cup dream, wherein I was standing at my Keurig in awe as my cup overflowed until I heard Luke 6:38 (NIV): "Give, and it will be given to you. A good measure, pressed down, shaken together and running over, will be poured into your lap. For with the measure you use, it will be measured to you."

The "pouring out" is more of God's alignment in our lives as unity is being sewn in families and then communities and so on from there. Terri was overcome with tears as her spirit bore witness to the essence of my dream. She and I have been having a lot of synergistic experiences. She says I am waking up her soul, lighting a fire in her. But she knows it is God pressing in on both her heart and mine.

I pray a closer relationship with the Lord for you, honey. I have prayed for Him to gently draw you back to the heart of worship. I know you will lead worship again. He has equipped you and called you. Your music is filled with a soulfulness that comes only from Him. And only you can sing it. (I had to bring the subject up again.)

You, my darling daughter, have been walking others home. Your light shines even on my path. I pray it will shine brighter as you press into God's gentle calling on your life.

I am here praying and declaring holy alignments in your life. Look for the divine signs. Capture them in your heart, and even with your camera, whenever you can. Nothing is random, and nothing is coincidental. Everything truly good is God. He is with you. He is for you. He is all around you.

Bless you this day and always.

I love you bunches!
Mom

P.S. I do believe there will be creative solutions forthcoming for the homelessness in our country. Even if some of the homeless are there by choice, I believe there will be a superb action plan for this desperate problem, which will turn their lives into something more meaningful. For now, if we can all reach out to those right in front of us, our love and compassion for others will ignite God's holy fires.

# How Precious You Are

A word fitly spoken is like apples of gold
In settings of silver.
(Proverbs 25:11 NKJV)

**April 19, 2022**

Hi Punkin,

I don't know how many days you'll have been away when you read this, but I know your family will be missing you. It's not that we saw your busy, hard-working, almost twenty-seven-year-old self frequently, but it was a peace to have you close by. The traffic from home to your Seattle apartment is barely manageable most days, though it is a short distance in miles.

I know there will come a time in the next few years where we will live—not just temporarily as we are now—some distance apart. Dad and I are serious about semi-retiring to a location with much less rainfall and a lot more sunshine. You have your own continued travel and relocation plans. I do hope we end up settling somewhere reasonably close to our children. Secretly, I hope you girls will follow us to our next hometown, but that may not be feasible with the jobs or businesses we each have going.

We may begin to have visits like I've had with my mom over the years where we capitalize on every minute together for two-week visits a few times a year. That will be a strange transition for us, won't it? Since you're such a traveler, I'm sure you will find us wherever we are, and I will make it a home for everyone. To my great joy will I make it Home. And all the days in between visits from you and Riss will be the days I wait for my children to come home.

On another note, I took a few days off from writing to you in order to clear out some emotional clogs. My writing journey has been an intermittent sort of spiritual root canal. Putting words on paper is both a satisfying relief and a painful extraction: a sort of draining of emotional abscesses. (I won't share much of the words from the time spent muddling through the weeds that had to be uprooted from my thinking processes.)

Part of the abscess, if you will, is a shame that I have not been able to hide my emotional wounds even as I've spent my adult life trying to reconcile them. I don't clearly know how those wounds look to others or if they perceive them at all. The best we can do as parents is walk through our healing journey with integrity. I hope I have done so, despite the emotional clutter through which I've had to sort and sift.

I regret to have been taught most often by hollow recitations—often gratuitous—on the subject of how much God loves us. *How* He loves us isn't often well explained. *That* He does is only a matter of fact in the mind of a person who already feels dearly loved and valued by others. Moreover, we understand so little of how He wants to heal us of our wounds. Jeremiah 30:17 speaks the word that God desires to restore our health and heal us of ALL our wounds.

I was sure my granny loved Jesus, and He her. But I was never certain there was enough love to go around, though I've heard many times, "Jesus loves you." It was easy to believe how much Granny and my mom loved me because I could *feel* it. Until recently, God's love did not have a feeling I could distinctly perceive in that tangible way.

I heard the Holy Spirit speak to my spirit about a year ago a message of profound love that I previously could not comprehend. He spoke to me about how precious I am/we are to the Lord. I have seen myself differently since then; I see myself more like God sees me. In seeing myself with God's eyes, I find it difficult to do something I did for decades, which was condemn myself.

The enemy's reign of terror over my life involved much condemnation.

I wrote this post on my private IG account where I've been practicing/publishing my writing. It seems fitting to share with you now:

I haven't always loved myself.

In fact, as a manifestation of a young life of trauma and much internalized anxiety, I loathed myself. I turned inward all the confusion and sorrow as I sought to survive chaos.

I've pulled off accomplishments and many days of a calm confidence, which defied my internal dialogue.

God has been revealing to me lately how precious we are to Him, how precious I am to Him.

Here's the thing:

God changes how you feel about yourself when you begin to understand how He sees you.

It is through His eyes that you learn just how precious you are and how easy it is then to give yourself GRACE, and to then give others grace.

Where there's no condemnation for self, there's none for others.

I wish we could look back on our lives and see the JOY, only the joy: the polka-dotted, barefooted, carefree summer days of endless joy.

But we naturally don't. We tend to let the pain and the sorrow and the trauma stick in our souls. It sticks until we recognize and rebuke the lies spoken over us. God's Word instructs us to bind and loose all that is not from Him. Freeing ourselves takes diligence in seeking our true Healer. It takes a new internal narrative about who we are called to be.

I'm on a journey back to myself. Not because I need to belong to myself, as the world would suggest, but because I'm listening carefully, intentionally, to what God says about me.

I belong to Him.

You belong to Him.

May His LOVE and GRACE and HEALING pour out on you today, that you would receive His overwhelming affection for you. He is always waiting to redeem and restore our hearts in Him.

Honey, it is my prayer for you today and every day that you will see yourself through God's eyes, that you will take back your whole life from any part of the enemy's remaining condemning grip. It is a deep pain as a parent to observe your child suffer in any way. This must be how God feels about His children who are believing the enemy's lies. It must break His heart.

Dear Jesus,

I ask today that You would pour out Your healing balm on Maddie's tender spirit. May she receive divine healing for all her emotional wounds, those deeper ones that everyone who travels this world shares in, and those that aren't so easily recognizable. I loose the self-condemning lies of the enemy from her soul; I bind the precious love of God to her, that she may feel and know how precious she is. In this new view of herself, may she treat herself with Your kindness and Your grace, always. Lord Jesus, reveal her preciousness to her, that she may experience the joy and freedom that comes with full acceptance of herself. Lord, I ask that she know deep in her spirit how valuable and loved she is. Pour out Your love and Your healing balm in all her broken places where the enemy has convinced her that she is inadequate, flawed, ashamed. Let her stand in Your great love today. Speak, Holy Spirit, to her clearly such that the love of Jesus pours into her and brings instant healing wherever it is needed. Thank You that she is in Your precious hands. She is the most precious thing to me. Thank You for revealing Yourself to her, for healing her in ways she may not even know she needs, and for always surrounding her with Your presence.

Amen.


Always here praying, with my heart full of love for you. I hope you *feel* God's love today.

XoXo,

Momma

# Disappearing Elk on a Nevada Highway
## Midnight Hour

Then Jesus told them, "I tell you the truth, if you have faith and don't doubt, you can do things like this and much more. You can even say to this mountain, 'May you be lifted up and thrown into the sea.' And it will happen." (Matthew 21:21 NLT)

**April 20, 2022**

Though I've told you the story of the disappearing elk, I share it again to recharge your faith. Your faith is intact, Maddie! And though it's been crowded out by the inundation of humanistic ideologies, cleverly packaged, often disguised, and expertly marketed to young people, your faith will arise.

Let this story of faith, which very well may have been a life-saving miracle, be strong evidence for God's miraculous intervention in our lives.

We were driving a rented SUV and towing Marissa's Tiguan when we encountered a herd of elk somewhere in the middle of a black night on a Nevada highway. There appeared five of them directly in front of our vehicle. They were boldly, unflinchingly standing firm while we inched toward them, unable to stop. I kid you not, honey, they were staring us straight in the eye. Dad was saying, "Oh no, oh no, oh no!" as he began slowly braking, trying to decide which elk was smallest and would do the least destruction. In a literal knee-jerk reaction, I started to cover my head with my pillow and pull my knees up to my chest, but then I pulled the pillow back down and cried out, "Lord Jesus, help us!" The elk vanished. They were not on the side of the highway; there was no movement; they were just gone.

Dad and I could not believe our eyes. We rode in silence for quite some time because the episode seemed unreal. We traveled many more miles down the dark highway on the edge of our seats, highly alerted to more elk crossing our path.

Your sister slept through the whole miracle and Dad's pants-pooping. I guess a year of college in Arizona was that exhausting.

A few weeks went by, but the event kept coming to mind, and I felt a message pressing on my spirit. I asked God to confirm His miracle for me. This is what the Holy Spirit said: "I am removing all obstacles from your path. I will not allow destruction to come your way. No matter how big or imminent disaster seems, I am bigger. I am your protector, and I can, and I will, and I have moved mountains, not just elk, for you. The more you see that I am there with you, the more you will see that I am there with you."

Remember how I used to repeat the line from *Veggie Tales*, "God is bigger than the bogeyman"? Well, He is. I may have mentioned that we are living in a time in history when numerous miracles are pouring out on God's people. The earth is truly filling with His Glory.

Glory = the light and power of God.

This verse dances off the page today:

> God's plan is to make known his secret to his people, this rich and glorious secret which he has for all peoples. And the secret is that Christ is in you, which means that you will share in the glory of God.
> (Colossians 1:27 GNT)

Heavenly Father,

I ask You to pour Your glory out on Maddie today. Let her experience Your power and Your light, that she may know it can be only You, Lord. Strengthen her in her faith, and loose from her soul all that is not from You. May You highlight for her the worldly ways in which she has innocently sought what feels like light and power. Reveal all deceptions to her, and lead her to truth through all that she ingests in her spirit, mind, and body. Thank You for gently drawing her back to You, Lord. Her destiny cannot be fulfilled without You. I declare today that she is rising up, adjusting her crown, and letting out a lion's roar as she walks in glory. Let gold-dust glory surround her so that she may fall at Your feet with immense gratitude for all the miracles You've done for her. She is Yours, Lord, but thank You that she is also ours. We love her so. Let her see how You are always there with her. Protect her, always, from the bogeyman. And move her mountains as she observes Your miracles all around her. Amen.

Love and prayers from home,

Ma

# Day 22

You will also DECLARE a thing,
And it will be established for you;
So light will shine on your ways.
(Job 22:28 NKJV, emphasis mine)


**April 22, 2022**

Dear Madz,

As I may have mentioned, I started on April 1, 2022, with the assignment to write to you for forty consecutive days. There is something biblical about doing anything for forty consecutive days. My (limited) understanding is that the forty days represent a sort of trial or probation period given over to the blessed end of a new beginning.

I got clogged up and overwhelmed, as I mentioned in a previous letter, with all I felt in my heart to share with you, so I took a few days off to recharge. I write freely most days, about 1,000 words, but the critic camped out on my shoulder and tried to convince me that you would find my writing unintelligent, cringey, and perhaps even useless.

Which words will speak to your heart from mine? Can I find them? Am I even capable?

I push through the doubt and the lies today and any concern with what you may/may not think as you read my words. I don't write to impress, to drop in my fifty-cent words (which Marissa refers to as my "party trick"). I write because it comes from my heart. I write because the language I speak ministers to the intended audience (though they remain largely undefined at this point) who relates to my *voice*. I write because I'm the only one who can tell my story.

Perhaps this exercise/assignment is partly to bring more light to the lies and curses of self-criticism/condemnation. If there's one thing that hurts me the most regarding you and Riss, it is hearing you speak against yourselves.

It's that same lying voice that wants us to play small while it says, "Who do you think you are?"

That voice is straight from the pit of hell. Use your words to send it back!

Who I think I am is someone who feels compelled to write and who desires to share my inner life with you as well as others.

And you know this, honey:

Words are the most powerful expressions of our thoughts.

Words are covenants; words are agreements.

Thoughts = Words = Actions = Results

(your basic life-coaching model/cognitive behavioral therapy)

I asked the Holy Spirit to speak to the ball of yuck called doubt/ fear/playing small today.

When your tongue is sharp against yourself, it is sharp against others. Do not use your words as swords *against* but as weapons *for*! Speak light and life and love into existence. Your words create heaven or hell on earth. Take them, each one, captive and make them obedient to what God says about you; if you don't know what God says about you, ask. What, Holy Spirit, do You say about Maddie today?

She is kind and warm toward others, but her spirit is sometimes weighted down with turmoil and confusion. Some of this is generational curses, lies, and proclivities toward pride. Pride is a cover for shame. Rebuke the shame and the pride will go. The fear of man/what others think drives a perfectionism that is a misguided focus. I shine My light on her spirit now, and I lead her out of this wilderness. Instruct her to write for forty days about her words and thoughts of herself, her fears and worries, so she can take them captive in order to rewrite them from a positive perspective. This forty-day assignment will bring her a new beginning. A girl will emerge who understands more of who she is in Christ. When she sees herself through her Father's eyes, she can no longer speak ill of herself, even in subconscious ways that may belie her intentions.

Assignments from a teacher-mom:

Read Jennie Allen's book *Get Out of Your Head*. (Re-read if you've already done so.)

Also, write about a topic for forty days consecutively, and then follow up with an analytical summary. Get quiet and allow God to speak to your heart. He so desires to do so and will honor your stepping in. A structure that works for me is to *step in* by praying and listening to soaking music, and then I begin typing or writing the first few words that come to mind. The words begin to quickly flow, often to the point where my typing fingers can barely keep up.

Also, I felt it impressed upon me just now that your journals of your time abroad will be made into a book. Perhaps we're both going to be real authors.

Cheers to that idea!

I sure do love you, Punkin.

Mom

P.S. On fifty-cent words: here's an old favorite from your dear old dad:

*Floccinaucinihilipilification*
Part of Speech: noun
Definition: the act of defining or estimating something as worthless

Origin: This word stems from the combination of four Latin words, all of which signify that something has little value: *flocci, nauci, nihili, pili*. This style of word creation was popular in Britain in the 1700s.

The meaning of the word itself ironically makes my point about fancy words.

# This Is Not Political

## It Is Biblical

Hang with me until the end . . .

The hopeful lenses of our eyes are fixed on the busy hands
of our dependable God. . . . He is working hardly
on our prayers. . . . Don't be afraid!
—Israelmore Ayivor, *The Great Hand Book of Quotes*

**April 24, 2022**

Dearest Maddie,

I enjoyed our Bounty Kitchen take-out dinner at your apartment
on Nob Hill. We surely wouldn't have planned to drive your direction
had we advance notice of Biden's arrival in Seattle that day. In the
jammed traffic, I could *feel* the spiritual darkness. I wondered what
business of the people the administration had, specifically in Seattle.

I do perceive a desperate attempt on the Biden administration's
part to further partner with any governors who will comply with

a dark agenda so they can carry out the plans as they've devised. I believe by the time you read this letter, there will be many who will have defected from Washington D.C.'s current agenda. The people of all parties are fighting back with a righteous anger, dissenting from faulty policies and cloaked agendas. There is forthcoming an exodus from both main political parties.

The global political agendas are still to be fully revealed. Perhaps our governor, who many believe is there fraudulently, will have been recalled. I believe every rightful politician will take their seat. Thieves will have to give back what they have stolen, and no amount of supposed conspiratorial accusations will cover their crimes.

To advance the agenda, *information itself* is being largely controlled; it may be the biggest propaganda campaign in history.

These are not my ideas; they are truths gleaned from news of a different source than mainstream media. They align with what I have perceived in my spirit, for several years now, to be an epic battle between Good and Evil. It was brewing long before Trump came into office. Trump threw a wild card wrench in the One World Order agenda. It's one reason people who find him distasteful held their noses and voted for him anyway.

I will insert here that whatever/whomever is "debunked" by the mainstream media is usually (perhaps always) someone who "has their number." Thus, someone/something on whom/which you should do your own independent research. As well, *who* they promote and *what* they promote is more of a mandate to scrutinize their "facts" and "fact checkers" than it is actual truth to be believed. (This, my love, is how propaganda works.)

They (i.e., the talking heads who are in control of the narrative) have attempted to silence some of our most brilliant voices. These voices are exceedingly wiser, and if you'll listen for yourself to someone they condemn, you may be quite surprised by what you discover as you engage your own discernment. Look for hyperbole, cheap shots, and name-calling, and there you will find sweeping lies told to run cover for truths they don't want you to see. While every human is flawed by nature and should never be held up as infallible, please also listen for common sense, logic, and truths that line up with your innermost wisdom. God is using the most unlikely people to carry out His plans. Listen carefully, judge discerningly, and vet everyone. Question your sensibilities, love! Keep in mind that you are being "sold" some things, and what's up is down, and what's down is up.

What I share may *sound* political, religious, conspiratorial, or just plain crazy. I share it anyway. I share it knowing there are those whom I love dearly, family and friends, whose eyes will roll back into their heads to read what I'm saying. (Those people may have stopped reading long before now.) I stand in a firm boldness, braced for whatever condemnation will ensue, because I know the truth will be revealed in time.

It is also difficult to express because many are challenged to think beyond Republican versus Democrat talking points or Left versus Right issues, even as both sides have mostly corrupt, self-serving agendas. I believe politicians work together across party lines to line their own pockets while they put on a show, running around with their hair on fire in exasperation of what the other side is doing. Again, it's often just an orchestrated show. The pitting of one politician or one party against another matters not, as each one is simply a character actor in a much larger story. The mostly contrived bantering has been a ruse for quite some time.

I don't doubt the truths that align with what is felt in my spirit. There is a quickening now of what is inevitable: God will move His hand on this earth, and life will never be the same. In all good ways, life will change, though it will be necessarily ugly getting there. I believe heartily in what God's chosen prophetic voices (which I vet within my own spirit) are declaring in these times.

So much I want you to be prepared for! But I trust God to care for you and all of my family as the earth rumbles in a necessary shakedown of life as we know it. Let freedom ring!

In a few weeks, we are going to a special showing of a movie called *2000 Mules*. It is a documentary about the people captured through geo-tracking who carried just one aspect of the massive voter fraud of 2020: stuffing ballot boxes. It's an important truth that will be fully revealed. Whether a person digs Trump or not will cease to be a talking point, as will the oft-repeated, carefully crafted "conspiracy theory" talking point. (Not to suggest conspiracy theories don't exist.) Any person who cares about freedom will be appalled as the truth unfolds. Check out 2000mules.com if you desire to do your own research. Decide for yourself.

Know that the Left, with all the media carrying their water, is now busy debunking the accuracy of geo-tracking, though there are many quotes on record from *them* about its precision. Oopsy-daisy.

Anyway, as we were crawling through the Seattle traffic on our way to have dinner, I felt inclined to pray in the spirit against the darkness I felt. When we finally were about to exit off the freeway and out of the main traffic jam, a double rainbow appeared through which a massive eagle flew. The eagle continued to fly alongside our vehicle for a mile or so.

Did you know God is pouring out His glory? Rainbows are a reminder of His promises. There are double and triple rainbows being reported everywhere, even when there is no rain. God is taking back His people, each and every precious one whom He loves, including everyone under the rainbow.

He's pouring out, healing hearts, and healing our land. Unity between race, gender, political class, etc. is being sewn like never before in our history. I don't see it yet, but I *feel* it gaining momentum. We will stand as one people in the revealed truth of how phony and disguised issues have been used to divide us. The hatred, bitterness, and resentment have been the destructive, sadly effective, and divisive goals of the massive propaganda.

We will soon find out that we have lived in a time of great lies. Praise God that truth pours out in His glory. We will look back at this time in our history to realize that we were all enslaved to a large extent. We've been living in a pantomime wherein a phony president, who is simply a front man, played, badly, an acting role.

One of the prophets I listen to calls it "The Greatest Show on Earth." He has a poignantly descriptive version of the characters in this particular circus.

Let this information in, though it may seem conspiratorial, so you can process what is happening in the earth. It is indeed biblical, quite literally.

On a lighter subject: I enjoyed walking around your apartment and observing your styling and little decorative touches. Your bedroom is also sweet and cozy. I look forward to pictures of your Sweden apartment and helping you when you return to the States, if you'll invite me, to style your next home. I hope the inspiration you gather will pour out all over me too.

I know you will adopt much of the Scandinavian style, as it is close to your natural style as evidenced in your serene bedroom at home that so many of our guests now enjoy. When I observe your style, I feel your kind and tender sensitivities to this world; I so much appreciate this aspect of you.

Dad and I also enjoyed seeing the Excel sheets you've created for Amazon. You undersell your many gifts and talents, but I stand in awe of how God has made you. You take in the world in a profoundly sensitive manner. I am looking forward to your "view" of Sweden, as your photography has such a special quality. What is it like to have an artist's eye so keen? I love looking through your lens.

Thank you, Lord Jesus, for Your truth and revelation. Thank You that You are pouring out on us no matter where we are, who we are, or what we understand about the spiritual matters unfolding in this world.

Bring us ALL together under the Big Top Circus tent! Let our true freedom ring!

And thank You, Jesus, that You are at work, always, answering all our prayers. Give Maddie faith in all that she asks and desires. Remind her today of what a big God You are and how precious she is.

Amen.

Bless you!,
Momma

P.S. I've started having visions. They come when my eyes are closed in prayer. The format is like a vertical comic strip in black and white, and usually there are three or four separate picture boxes before the vision ends. I recently had this vision: Box 1: Biden is on the television standing at a podium. Box 2: The television screen goes completely black. Box 3: A football referee appears, making the illegal pass and illegal shift motions. (I had to research what I was seeing, as I did not know well these football referee signals.) Box 4: The television screen goes black again.

# What Do You Do with Frustration and Disappointment?

Listen to advice and accept discipline,

    and at the end you will be counted among the wise.

Many are the plans in a person's heart,

    but it is the Lord's purpose that prevails.

(Proverbs 19:20–21 NIV)

## April 25, 2022

Does your emotional pendulum swing wide, with no in-between, from segments of joy and peace to hopelessness?

In her aforementioned book, *Get Out of Your Head*, Jennie Allen says each of the lies we believe about ourselves falls into one of these three categories:

I'm helpless.

I'm worthless.

I'm unlovable.

Did you know it's incredibly painful as a parent to hear your child speak unkindly of herself? Many of us are prone to turning our frustrations inward and becoming our own enemy.

Jennie says, "Every lie we buy into about ourselves is rooted in what we believe about God."*

What do you believe about God?
What do you believe about yourself?

If you can thoroughly and honestly answer these questions, you will have instruction in proceeding forward without the burden of perfectionism and shame that sometimes drives emotions and reactions.

Our minds can be our friend or our enemy. The devil is always fighting for control of our thoughts because every aspect of our lives is a manifestation of them.

Thought control is the tool the enemy uses to keep us playing small, hiding out, missing our destiny, and from sharing the love and power of God in us with others.

I am concerned about the propaganda that is being peddled in our schools (and all over the world). But how could I, as a teacher, suggest that some teachers in our education systems are part of the problem?

---

* Jennie Allen, *Get Out of Your Head: Stopping the Spiral of Toxic Thoughts* (Colorado Springs, CO: WaterBrook, 2020), 15.

Teachers have become cynics.

Parents have become adversaries.

Students have become numbers rather than individuals.

There is little education, but big propaganda.

A cynicism pervades our education system.

Bless all the many teachers who have risen above the noise to serve the true needs of their students.

I'm seeing my own teaching career with new eyes, hearing with new ears. It's all a bit unfamiliar, and yet the world makes more sense every day.

Well, that was a strange installment of my writing.

Take it for what it is.

I believe I've already mentioned to read Jennie Allen's book.

I love you, my firstborn. And if you were just another brick in the wall, I'd love you to the ends of the earth anyway. I'm glad you're not, and I'm glad you're ours.

Much love! Big hugs!

I hope you find some humor or *something* in my words.

# On Full Circles and Coffee Shops and How God Speaks to Hearts

The Lord will send a blessing on your barns and on everything you put your hand to. The Lord your God will bless you in the land he is giving you. (Deuteronomy 28:8 NIV)

## May 2, 2022

I received a prophetic word from Pastor Nathan that I was being called to a place of open fields with horses running free. He specifically saw me in a field near a tractor, where there was a house and many horses. He also saw a large red barn out in the field. I believe this was a vision of the life I left behind in Montana. He then said I would be going back to my roots, which he said would lead to increased creativity and going to the next level, spiritually speaking. He said, "God is pouring out on you because your heart is ready."

I already had a trip to Montana planned to see family. It is pressed on my heart how God is sowing/sewing a thread of unity in our family, with me at the helm. (Imagine that.)

I returned to Montana after eight years of not traveling due to the reign of terror over my health, of which you are keenly aware. One afternoon during my visit, when Uncle Hoss was driving me along a stretch of road near my alma mater, I spotted a large red barn that has likely been there decades. My attention was drawn to it for the first time, though I had likely driven by hundreds of times many years earlier. I snapped a picture of the barn as confirmation of God's word to me.

Big old red barns can become ordinary when you live in rural Montana, but how beautiful they are when they bring your heart back home. Even more so when they confirm God's hand in your life.

Honey, I so treasure the watercolor you painted of this red barn. Please paint for me always.

Tying this all together, I had been having thoughts that it would be fun to work in a coffee shop. Shortly thereafter, the Holy Spirit revealed to me He wants me to open my own coffee shop. I wasn't sure this was what I was hearing. I had no plans, even vague ones, to open any kind of business.

A few days after the coffee shop idea was planted in my spirit, I was praying about something else when I heard, "Full Circle Coffee Company: it's a heart thing. You will return home to family; it will be a full circle moment, of many full circles to come. I am giving you the key to door number 51; it will unlock earthly riches." I woke up at 5:10 that day. (My birthday is 10/5!) I wrote for an hour or so as I usually do. Later that day, I felt to write again, though I don't usually write in the afternoon. I looked at the clock just as I finished my writing to see it was 5:10, again. God then spoke into my spirit: "This is a circle within a circle, as a clock is a circle, and I am bringing you full circle. I am giving you back what the enemy has robbed from your life. The locust years are over now."

I don't have full revelation of what the numbers and symbols God uses mean, but He's talking and I'm listening. (He speaks to us all in such unique ways.) When researching even biblical interpretation of numbers or symbols, you can probably find whatever meaning suits you. It's always best to trust the Holy Spirit as your continual guide, lest you fall down an internet rabbit hole.

As if it weren't enough confirmation, simultaneous to writing out how this full circle idea was unfolding, I was listening to a prophet speaking online. He said, "According to Psalm 51, God is opening a door of revelation as we stop blaming ourselves, and receive/give forgiveness."

Also, as another thought of interest, our first house number here was 1510. I believe Dad and I have been taken back to the first years of our marriage in order that our relationship can be fully healed and restored. More circles in time. Sometimes you have to go back to go forward.

How can this not be a redemption story?

Weeks later, I had the dream previously mentioned wherein I was standing at my Keurig coffee machine, pressing the button for my morning coffee. The coffee began to pour out and would not stop. As it ran over the cup and all over the butler's pantry, I simply stood in amazement. I didn't rush to clean it up; I just watched it pour out. As soon as I woke up from the dream, I heard remnants of a verse

I knew from many years ago. "Full measure, good measure, pressed down and running over." And then He said, "I have brought you out of dry deserts. Great is My faithfulness to you and your family. Let Me. Rest. It is done. Breathe. Create. All good things are yours: full measure, a good measure, pressed down and running over."

I was then prompted to look up the actual verse in Luke 6:37–38 (NIV): "Do not judge, and you will not be judged. Do not condemn, and you will not be condemned. Forgive, and you will be forgiven. Give, and it will be given to you. A good measure, pressed down, shaken together and running over, will be poured into your lap. For with the measure you use, it will be measured to you." He then said, "These will be the years you will count as joy."

As incredible confirmation, last weekend at our conference in Bend, Oregon, we were given what are called words of knowledge from two different people who were perfect strangers. On the day's drive to the conference, Dad and I had brainstormed coffee shop business ideas, as my dreams have sparked our next adventure.

Here are the words, independently given, from two different people in attendance:

"You two are about to go on a joy ride!"

"I don't know what business idea you two have *brewing*, but it is going to be massively successful and filled with God's blessings."

"Get going because God is all over it!"

I should hang out with these sorts of people more often.

It might also interest you to know this word for me, specifically, which was from the guy sitting in my row at the conference. After almost two days of sitting near each other but talking no more than friendly greetings, he popped this off (paraphrased to the best of my memory):

I think I have a word for you. If you're not already having dreams and visions, God is going to give them to you. If you are, He's going to give you more of them. You are going to be doing some teaching, even prophetically, using just one word to unpack God's Word for people. You will speak with your own unique perspective and ideas, and not just say what others say.

Also, I feel like you two (to me and Dad both) are moving. I don't like to say *where* when I have words of knowledge, but it feels like Montana. And whatever you two have planned, God is all over it.

He then told Dad he must think outside the box in wrapping up his business (and our lives here in Washington.)

Sounds like a book and a coffee shop and many full circles in time. I'll maybe tell you in another letter about how the full circle concept first came to me in visions of wagon wheels, another tie to Montana.

If you don't have your own business by the time ours is built, we'd very much like to have you work with us. The job will require two things: a little knowledge about lattes and a BIG heart for people.

You're more than qualified, Barista Maddie.

Have a good cup of Swedish coffee today, and send me a pic.

Cheers to coffee breaks and coffee shops.

All the love,
Momma

# A Retro Letter on Your Golden Birthday

> Blessed is she who has believed that the Lord
> would fulfill his promises to her!
> (Luke 1:45 NIV)

**May 27, 2022**

Dear Madison Suzanne,

It's your Golden Birthday! Wow, twenty-seven years! I love you, my girl!

I wrote the following letter for you when you were a senior in high school. I recently found my handwritten rough draft tucked in some household paperwork. I don't remember which assignment you were given that required a letter from me about you. I do recall plunking it out rather quickly and surprising myself with such a quick summary of who you were at that time in your life. I think you'll get a kick out of reading it almost exactly ten years after it was written. It's all still true, and not much has changed. (And I still reserve my somewhat shameless bragging rights because my parental pride is in my heart and not my head. It is not so much for what I've done as your momma, but for who God has made you to be. I'm so grateful to Him!)

Here it is:

Maddie is an intrinsically motivated young woman who stands on her principles. She is a girl of substance and high moral character who quietly but strongly reflects leadership and commitment to her goals, beliefs, and the well-being of others. While she is a strong leader, she is also a team player who can bridge a divide between others. Her friends often seek her counsel and refer to her as "Switzerland" for her ability to be neutral when emotions are strong.

She has a ready and welcoming smile that reflects a deep regard and compassion for others. She delivers many little thoughtful acts of kindness, such as handmade cards with heartfelt sentiments to celebrate the special occasions of those she cares about.

While she is an extremely hard worker, she is also a creative musician who balances her serious, introspective side with art, music, and an abundance of humor.

She is well-rounded and enjoys challenges and new adventures but deeply values home, God, family, and friends.

Bless you this day, my baby girl, with an amazing Golden Birthday! I pray your friends would come through with the same tender thoughtfulness you offer to them. The Lord is fulfilling His promises in you. You are a blessing and a treasure to be held dear!

Cheers to twenty-seven years, Golden Girl!

You are so loved.
Ma

# A Dream about Dreams

And they were canopied by the blue sky,
So cloudless, clear, and purely beautiful,
That God alone was to be seen in Heaven.
—Lord Byron

## June 2, 2022

Oh hey Swedie (you must be feeling more Swedish by now),

Here's another of my night dreams:

I dreamed of a winding path filled with people's hopes and dreams. The dreams were represented as either little black or blue squares. The squares seemed like both books and large external hard drives. I felt a distinct impression in the dream as I moved along the path that Obama was finding out that he wasn't the king of the universe. He was no longer going to be able to control what people could have/do, essentially what dreams they could hold for their lives. I knew the dreams represented in blue were of the Lord, while the black ones had to wither on the vine.

As mentioned, I plan to take a biblically based dream interpretation course in the near future. For now, here is my armchair interpretation:

I believe God is renewing the dreams He put in our hearts from the beginning. He is setting us on a new path of discovery, a discovery of our WHOLE selves. He is making us whole in Him, discarding lies/curses while bringing His redemption to our lives.

God is simultaneously striking down emperors and kings—self-appointed dictators—as He exposes them for their deeply evil plans. Soon, the emperor will have no clothes. I have believed this about Obama for some years. The first time I saw him on TV, the hairs on the back of my neck stood up. (I think you know this.) Prepare for a revealing of sinister plans in which he is inextricably involved. His great exposure is coming!

> For the Lord is our judge, the Lord is our lawgiver, the
> Lord is our king; he will save us.
> (Isaiah 33:22 KJV)

Whether Trump is destined to come back or not, I will say events of biblical proportions are on the horizon. Beautiful blue horizons. In the waters and in the skies, we will be surrounded with true blue redemption.

This isn't about Obama, Trump, or any other leader. I can appreciate how this is all sounding to your ears. But it's too important not to share with you. Forgive me now and thank me later, honey. Please give me all your grace, and hang on to your seat.

Really though, how can one share these ideas when both politics and religion have become so inflammatory? And when the very same spirit of self-righteousness rules them both?

Wouldn't it be amazing if we could more often express and receive ideas in a genuine way with one another? We may find that we are more aligned, more in agreement, and more like each other. Unfortunately, a carefully devised plan to divide has been working incredibly well, even in families, for quite some time now, with each "side" screaming at the other and nobody hearing or listening to anything but what comes from their own megaphone. And wasn't that the point to creating "sides" in the first place: positions of thought propped up by perpetual outrage, beguiling talking points, and often under the guise of key societal issues? Legitimate issues perhaps, but beside the point of their supposed premise.

It gives me a chuckle as I point out again that I taught you girls not to ever discuss religion or politics at school, and here I am expressing what seems like a lot of both in an actual book to you. I did not want you to get shouted down or bullied if you expressed a differing point of view than the ones with the biggest proverbial microphone. It was also to help you avoid divisive arguments with those who do not seek understanding, those who would rather cram an idea down until others acquiesce. It's sad how often this approach to important issues has pervaded our society.

And why are we so sensitive to listening to another's point of view with which we disagree? Is our truth that fragile? How did we, as a society, lose all good manners and respectful communication methods such that we cannot honor another person's perspective? And why are we preaching to our choirs when it only further divides us from those who can truly help us expand our narrow minds?

I take great hope that we are going to experience unity in the United States and in the whole earth as we all soon discover we are on the same side of freedom.

Speaking of perspectives, horizons, and blue skies, I know you'll capture many sunsets while you're in Sweden and in the other countries you'll visit as well. Have you been noticing for quite some time how unique and interesting the cloud formations are? Have you noticed the multi-colored sunsets and sunrises? I have heard the sky is often pink in Sweden.

I believe God is teaching His people to look up. I repeat: the warring in the heavens will be won by the forces for Good. I have a distinct sense that truths undeniable will be written across the skies. I don't know how or when. I just know to pay attention, to look up. I know science cannot explain the supernatural, though science is God's creation as well.

This day, as you look up, I know you will also be living out the dream in your heart to live in Europe. So many talk about such adventures, but few find the courage to live them.

I'm so, so proud of you. And I miss you like the dickens!

Dream on.

Look up.

Get ready for victories.

*Love you bunches and gobs!*

*Mom*

# She Came Dancing in on Ribbons of Light

He heals the brokenhearted
and binds up their wounds.
(Psalm 147:3 NIV)

**June 3, 2022**

Dear Maddie,

Last March, Callie came to me in a dream. She was twirling and swirling on vibrant turquoise and magenta ribbons of light. She said, "Momma, can I lay my head on your chest? I need to pray for your heart." I picked her up and held her close so her head could rest on my heart. She seemed to be six or seven years old, almost too tall to cradle. I had a distinct sense that my heart was being healed in every way, including the physical damage from the heart attack but also for all the times I felt broken, sad, defeated. Callie prayed and then skipped off to be with my aunt Kris, who came toward me. I started to say to my auntie how she should be so proud of her granddaughter, but then I realized Callie is Aunt Kris's great-niece, not her granddaughter. Without saying so, both conveyed that Aunt Kris is taking care of Callie until her own grandma comes to heaven. They were filled with joy and had so much love for one another.

When I woke up from the dream, I realized Aunt Kris went to heaven when Callie would have been almost seven years old. It was such confirmation to me that our baby Callie and our beloved aunt Kris are indeed together in heaven.

I have such hope for heaven. And I don't know if Callie visited me or I was transported to her. I do know the ribbons were made of the brightest lights and most vibrant colors I've ever seen. Callie was filled with joy as she swirled and twirled and delivered such love with her very presence.

I know my heart is healing.

And the spirit of grief has left me now.

I wonder how Callie's death has really affected you deep in the layers of your soul. Though you were only five when she died, I know you struggled to process not only the loss and disappointment that we came home from the hospital with no baby sister, but also the grief that pervaded our home for so long after.

You asked Dad one day, "When is Momma going to stop crying?"

Your self-imposed therapy was your "artist-ing" (still my favorite of your "little kid" words). For many months after, you drew pictures and wrote stories, addressing many of them to Callie. Fortunately, I have saved many of your creations, and though there is a sadness in the reminders of that time, there is also a fierce resiliency to make sense of life, to creatively speak the pain out along with the love.

Walking you through your grief helped me walk through mine.

I pray the deepest parts of your heart are being fully healed. I honor you for all you've been through. I pray this day that the love of Jesus will come twirling and swirling on ribbons of light all over your beautiful life.

Even though Callie looks down from heaven, I know she looks up to you, her big sister.

All my love, from the very bottom of my (healing) heart,

Momma

# Sharing a Letter about My Granny

A letter written for my granny, slightly modified today
(read by Brett, at Granny's Memorial Service, June 2019)

**June 7, 2022**

---

**In Memory of Bernadine Rita**
**1/31/24 – 6/18/19**

No one could belch (or poofer) louder than Granny or excuse themselves so politely. Sometimes she'd say, "Oh Angie!" as if the sounds she made came from elsewhere or that she was somewhat surprised herself. She was always inadvertently, innocently funny.

I was blessed by time spent with Granny, both in Minnesota during some of my very young years and in Montana during my high school and college years. She was the best listener I know. I would walk the two-mile stretch of dirt road from our ranch to her little farmhouse across the highway just to talk. She would listen for hours and then give me a ride back home. She would always remind me how much Jesus loves us. Those deeply sincere words coming from her were a soothing balm to my spirit.

---

The many Sundays we went to church together changed my life, though I didn't perceive it at the time. We often went on Wednesday nights too. It was an Assembly of God, after all.

On the way to church, Granny always offered me the other half of her stick of gum. The smell and taste of Doublemint gum will forever remind me of her.

The sincere way she praised the Lord and with such surrender to her faith is etched in my heart. My own love for Jesus and the constant source of strength He's been in my life is largely owed to Granny's testimony, even though, as a younger version of myself, I thought she was a little gaga over Jesus.

I accepted the Lord at the Assembly in Granite Falls, Minnesota, when I was nine at a Wednesday night church meeting of my granny's invitation. I got baptized that year, and I know she must have been so pleased. As for me, a shy introvert with social anxiety, standing there dripping wet, freshly baptized on the stage up front, I was asked how I came to know Jesus, but I froze when the microphone was held up to my mouth. The audience chuckled warmly. But I wanted to shout, "My grandma!"

Again, in high school, at the Assembly in Laurel, Montana, I rededicated my heart to Jesus. I wept as I knelt at the altar. Granny was there then as well. It was always Granny in her unwavering faith, in her steadfast love for all of us. Because she was the real deal, what my family likes to call a Heart Christian. She truly loved with the love of Jesus. She didn't preach, she didn't judge, she truly loved.

Those early years in Minnesota were so important in my life, but the years we shared with Granny in Montana were an instrumental part of who I am today and, consequently, who my children are. Both of my girls are Heart Christians. Their genuine love and compassion for others reaches many. It can all be traced back to Granny.

She was truly on a mission. And it goes to my belief that we all always have a mission field right in front of us if we choose to recognize God's calling on our hearts.

As a side note, many of you may not know I gave her the nickname "Granny," which became everyone's term of endearment for her. She wasn't fond of it at first. She qualified it by saying only I could call her "Granny" because I was extra special (though I know she felt that way about all people). Then my high school track team started calling her Granny. "Thanks, Granny!" they'd say as she brought us freshly made raspberry bismarcks to enjoy after our track meets. I know how early in the morning she got up to bake fresh doughnuts for us. It was a gift from her heart, and baking was truly her art.

I owe much of my baking inspiration to her, and the rest to my momma. This week, coincidentally (or not), I have a baking gig for a wedding event. Baking has become part of my art as well, though I'll never be Granny or Mom or Aunt Deb. I come from a long line of bakers, and I'm proud of that. They say it's a lost art, but I will keep it going and pass it on. This week's pastries and cupcakes will be dedicated to Granny. So I am home baking while you honor Granny, but I'm with you in spirit.

Granny was our endearing *and* enduring cheerleader and a mighty prayer warrior for so many. How blessed are all who knew her.

It is my high honor to be her firstborn granddaughter.

She was Love.
She was Light.
She was Granny to many.

Her spirit, her joy, her warmth will forever resonate in our lives.

She will rest with angels and continue to bless us, her family, each one.

I love you, my granny.
Rejoice! You are home!

Sweetie,

I have a special cross-stitch quilt saved that Granny made for you when you were born. It was the last quilt she made before needlework got too tedious for her. Her work was impeccable, just as her baking was. Like us, she liked to create things with her hands, and everything she touched was beautiful. Now you know where you get it.

# A Forgiveness Letter to Dad

## (to follow)

Create in me a pure heart, O God,
  and renew a steadfast spirit within me.
(Psalm 51:10 NIV)

**June 8, 2022**

Sweetie,

I pray these words will bring healing redemption to the tender layers of your soul that may house the inevitable overflow of the mostly quiet war zone in which you sometimes lived as a child.

My biggest regret is engaging/disengaging with Dad in unhealthy ways that may have brought pain, even if indiscernible, to you and Riss.

I forgive myself now.

Please forgive me for all the times I lived in a sorrow and regret that tried to swallow me whole.

I wasn't my best.

Please remember all the times I was.

I have done all my best *things* with my girls in mind.

Thank you for the inspiration that comes from just being you.
You are the blessing of my life.

I love you BIGGER than all of it.

*All my love,*
*Momma*

Before you read my letter to Dad, here's a word from him:

---

Hi Mads,

Mom asked me for permission to include a very personal letter she wrote to ME as part of her letters to YOU. She was making a choice to forgive the many ways I truly abused her heart by my selfish and destructive behaviors over many years. You and Riss can both attest to my inner demons that I gave license to control so many family occasions and daily exchanges. Although I've not yet made everything right with your mom, I feel that this letter is important to share so you and your sis can witness true grace in action. It will become the main reason that we were able to rewrite our story as your parents and as a couple. I hope reading your mother's decision to forgive me and seeing all she had to overcome just to consider doing it will help you understand how hard she has worked to keep our little family intact. My refusal to see my own brokenness made me an insensitive and cruel adversary rather than a trustworthy partner for a wife and mother who only wanted to live a joy-filled life.

I feel humbled and appreciative for her gift of forgiveness to me. Her story would be incomplete without including this significant aspect of our family life. I am grateful to her and to God for the chance to correct course and become the man all three of my girls deserve. It's because of your mother's integrity and character that I am getting the opportunity to recreate my own.

Cherish these letters, sweetie. You are blessed to have a mother who loves her family so much that she deferred her dreams to make sure you had the support to pursue all of yours.

I love you very much.

Dad

**Forgiveness Tour**

Culminating Project, Wherein Bitter Roots Are Extracted
and We Are Both Released

> Do not judge, and you will not be judged.
> Do not condemn, and you will not be condemned.
> Forgive, and you will be forgiven.
> (Luke 6:37 NIV)

March 31, 2022

Dear Kevin,

Just to call you "dear" is quite an act of grace.

For forty consecutive days this past winter, I wrote on the subject of forgiveness. I delineated in my writings, sometimes with venom, much of the unpleasant, specific violations for which I choose to forgive you. The ugly past had to be excavated in order to move forward.

Many years ago, I decided to forgive you, even before you took any responsibility for your destructive behaviors. It was a determined, decisional forgiveness that was not yet able to take hold in my heart.

For my inability to feel any more grace for you, I condemned myself, which served the wrong master and only watered the bitter roots of unforgiveness.

I misunderstood God's concept of forgiveness and took those roots of bitterness up as my weapons against your incoming enemy fire.

I forgive you for doing the enemy's work, albeit unknowingly, to kill, steal, and destroy blessings, favor, and all fruits that could have been part of our lives and our family's lives. I forgive you for all you robbed from me, personally (though I quite understand just how impersonal it all was). I forgive myself for allowing you such unhealthy access to me.

I forgive you for the locust years where the pestilence of a leviathan spirit reigned in our home; I forgive myself for doing all the wrong things in my efforts to rise up against it. It was a giant that could not be slain with my little slingshot.

As I forgive you (formally), I also forgive myself for all the ugly ways I coped that only brought more pain to the situation.

Forgiveness, though not dependent on your actions, is tremendously aided by your willingness today to surrender your brokenness to God. I honor your journey toward wholeness.

This Forgiveness Tour has been a journey through a vast wilderness wherein I set down my weapons so I could take God's hand as He poignantly instructed me to do. This venture has been a direct assignment from God. Without much notice, He gave the due date for this culminating letter: today.

When I began the journey as an act of obedience to God's leading, the thought of a forgiveness letter was a sort of get-out-of-jail-free card for you because I hadn't fully reconciled the injustices lived out in our marriage. I understand now, through many synergistic teachings and divine revelations, that I am letting us both out of jail. And the "free" part refers to the vast, overflowing grace, love, and forgiveness of our heavenly Father.

So here I am to say:

I forgive you, Kevin. I release you, and I release me, from all trespasses and debts against me, against us, and against God.

Instead of belaboring past grievances, as I've often done in my struggle toward a deeper understanding of all the pain, I simply want to share with you some of what I've learned about forgiveness along the way. I took notes as I was instructed to do. I've been a real tourist on my own journey, capturing moments of beauty and truth, so I can always remember how to walk through forgiveness and into the grace that is available for us all. Our obedience brings forth great Holy Spirit revelations.

And so it is, as the gift of forgiveness naturally brings, that I walk a new path into a fresh alignment with God's divine plan over my life. I continue to see old things in new ways and new things that I had not eyes for previously. I decree this new and creative vision for both of us.

A big discovery was how difficult it was to forgive myself. On my journey back to me, I found a young girl buried in a pile of rubble, vehemently fighting back tears because crying felt like submission to the false authority in her life. She was broken and overpowered, and she despised herself for it. She was necessarily feisty and yet increasingly untrue to her nature and, therefore, her true purpose and destiny.

I didn't like her anymore, and that broke my heart the most. I picked up her pieces one day, dusted her off, and told her how much I honor her journey. I saw her how God sees her, and that changed everything.

Perhaps what informed me most about the concept of forgiveness was when Pastor Darren said (in a sermon delivered about halfway into my tour), "Who do you think you are to receive God's forgiveness for all you've ever done and yet hold fast to your judgment of someone else?" (You may also recall the part of the message where Pastor Darren said, "Some of you are tethered to 1987." And I knew before he finished that sentence that he would prophetically call out the year we got married.)

We cannot receive forgiveness freely if we cannot offer it, no qualifiers, and no exceptions.

I finish this assignment out with some Holy Spirit highlights from The Tour.

Day 33 brought a notable heart shift. Here's my download from that day (God is giving me rest now.):

There remains therefore a rest for the people of God.
(Hebrews 4:9 NKJV)

Together we have rescued the girl from the rubble. With your diligence and obedience and My powerful grace, love, and mercy, she is plucked from the rubble, from the enemy's pile of lies and deceptions and dirty, dusty tricks. Those tricks are old and dusty now, and you are wise to them. I surround you with My sword and My shield. I hide you in My Secret Place; therefore, no harm can come to you. Keep My Word (it is a new sword) in your heart, and you will carry My strength and My protection against all evil and toward greater healing and restoration. Yes, you are undergoing a restoration of extraordinary measures. I am in every detail. The more you see Me, the more you see Me! I surround you, as you request of Me, to fill every space within you and every space you're in. Omnipresent I Am. Enter My rest. It's been a dirty, grueling tour, but more light is breaking through, and you will finish well these last seven days.

On the fortieth day, this verse was highlighted for me:
Behold, I will do a new thing,
Now it shall spring forth;
Shall you not know it?
I will even make a road in the wilderness
And rivers in the desert.
(Isaiah 43:19 NKJV)

Download (on wilderness journeys):

You thought you deserved little, that you were not even truly worthy of My love. But it is My love that has sustained you and brought you through the wilderness and dry, cracked deserts of your life. It is My glory that pours out on you and your family now. You have asked, you have sought, and you have boldly knocked. I answer! Every day for the rest of your earthly life will be a day where I give back something the enemy robbed from you. Sometimes it will be small incremental blessings, just as some things were taken from you in often undiscernible but constant ways; other times, I will pour out a blessing so big you'll wonder how to contain it. Don't contain it! Share it! Your life will be an even greater blessing to others as you stand in My healing and My glory. I am using you, mightily, in the Third Great Awakening. It is here, and you are ready. Be bold, be strong, for the Lord your God is with you! Rivers of My living water pour out over you and your home and your family. My Spirit fills you and all the spaces you're in. I am taking you—I remind you—from glory to glory. This is a heart thing: a heart healing, a heart restoration, and a heart ministry. You, mighty little one, will minister to hearts. It is your natural bent given you in your mother's womb. You are a child of the Most High God. Adjust your crown today.

God sends me another postcard to the wilderness:

Loose unforgiveness and bitterness, ALL, from your soul. Bind My love and grace to your kind spirit.

My glory surrounds you, day and night. My glory surrounds all the places you are in and all the places within you. My glory holds all the keys to healing and restoration, and I pour it out on your thirsty soul. The roots are rotten, and they are being extracted; this is a spiritual root canal. It doesn't feel good while it's happening, but such relief will come. Relief in the form of peace. I am Peace. I remind you that I am taking you from glory to glory. Day and night, night and day, let your incense arise, let your praise arise. Our hearts are connected, and nothing can come between. I protect you from all evil. Worship My holy name.

I'll close with these truths:
I forgive you
Sincerely.
I love you
Dearly.
I appreciate you
Greatly.
I honor your journey back to yourself
Prayerfully.
I honor your journey back to God
Most of all.

We belong to God.

I speak healing over all aspects of our lives. His abundance is pouring out in new measures.

And.

I forgive you, Dear Kevin.

With love and grace and forgiveness,

Angie

Give, and it will be given to you. A good measure, pressed down, shaken together and running over, will be poured into your lap. For with the measure you use, it will be measured to you.

(Luke 6:38 NIV)

# Letter No. 27

## Culminating Project

You don't have to see the whole staircase,
just take the first step.
—Martin Luther King Jr.

**June 9, 2022**

What a dream I had last night as I fell asleep praying about whether
to give you the letters I wrote for you. As you've ascertained by now,
I've been having some interesting dreams. The symbolism God uses
to speak to us is quite profound and often beyond our own wisdom
and understanding of this world He created for us.

My prayer as I drifted off to sleep went something like this:

Lord Jesus, as my body rests, speak to my spirit with Your wisdom
and guidance as I decide whether to give Maddie her letters or not. I
have lost peace about the project, and I don't know if it's because they
are important for her, so the enemy is running interference, or if I'm
just doubting myself as I've been prone to do. I do not doubt You,

Lord, and Your higher wisdom. So impart in my spirit a clarity about the project, that I may wake with clear direction. Send the scribe angels to help me make any revisions to the letters before I print them. Thank you for helping me convey the deeper parts of my heart, and Yours, to my precious daughter. Amen.

I woke up with a clear directive to polish up the letters, revise a few things, and print them off for you.

At first glance, my dream didn't seem significant. Later in the day, as I shared the dream with Dad, confirmations began to unfold.

The dream:

I dreamed you, Dad, and I pulled into a garage sale, but there was no sign posted. So I don't know exactly how we knew it was a garage sale. It was a drizzly, cloudy, Northwest day. We were looking at the deck furniture cushions on the front deck of the house, explaining to you that these were the items we wanted to add to our new deck. The homeowner came out, and I expected him to be angry with us for trespassing on his front deck since no Garage Sale sign was posted. Instead, he was friendly and welcoming, so we asked him if he would consider selling us the cushions. He started in on a sales pitch about the particular cushions, and I concluded that he was not giving deals on them, nor did I want to hear what he had to say. I had the impression he sold these cushions for a living. I wanted them because they looked so comfortable. I thought you kids could sleep under the stars on our deck on these thick, almost bed-like cushions.

We told him he had already told us all about the cushions when we were there at a previous garage sale. We then left him standing there pitching the cushions while we went inside to look at what now seemed like a moving sale. You went back to the car after we showed you the cushions and waited for us there. Francis seemed to appear in the dream just as Dad and I entered the door off the deck. There was a staircase straight ahead of the door to access the main floor of the home. I took off in that direction to discover the staircase only went halfway up before it hit a dead-end wall.

I looked behind me to see that Francis and Dad were scaling what looked like a rock-climbing wall where indentations had been carved in the sheetrock for foot placement. As well, there were some wooden handles strategically placed for handgrips. Next to the foot placement slots were Post-it Notes with step-by-step instructions on how to scale the wall up to the main living area of the house where the sale items were. Francis and Dad just walked right up the wall without a thought while I tried to explain to them, because I felt silly, that I had followed the logical path up the stairs straight ahead of the entry door. I feared I could not scale the wall, but then I focused in on the directions on the Post-it Notes and realized that if I just took it one step at a time, following the instructions, it was very doable.

When we all got up to the main floor, we could see that there were many vintage pieces of furniture for sale, all looking nearly new, from the '40s, '50s, and '60s. The house was bright, spotlessly clean, and had a very cheerful energy. They had baby toys and games and vases and other housewares for sale as well. There were specific baby toys you had when you were little. It felt a bit like a time-capsule-stroll through decades of time.

I was looking for a specific type of dining table for you. They had many tables, lots of charming vintage pieces, but I left empty-handed because they did not have the one I was looking for.

Significant points:

We walked away from the "salesman" in the dream.

The staircase was a dead end, but it was the logical way to ascend.

I feared entering by way of the rock-climbing wall, but as soon as I surrendered to following the step-by-step directions, focusing only on each specific direction, I put one foot literally in front of the other and easily traveled up the wall to the main living area.

Francis and Dad ascended the wall as if they didn't even see the staircase, like it was the usual thing to do.

Once I got upstairs, the world seemed so much brighter as a cloudy day became a sunny day.

You were with us, but after hearing the sales pitch, you returned to the car to wait for us.

I was looking for a table for you.

I didn't find it.

I wasn't sure how we could get furniture down the wall anyway, if that was the route we had to take back out.

I saw toys that reminded me of your childhood: some that were the exact toys you had, all in like-new condition.

Everything was clean and shiny.

There were a lot of people there, and a happy chatter resonated throughout the house.

My thoughts on the dream (professional dream analysis pending):

In some larger sense, I have been inviting you, my dear daughter, to the table. In the dream, you had an openness to come along, and yet you returned to the car as soon as the sales pitch started. It was a drizzly, gray day, but when we got up to the main floor of the house, it was filled with a radiant joy. It was a moving sale (a few days before your move to Sweden) with a museum quality. It walked me through the decades of your childhood years, which were playful, light-hearted, and filled with much happy chatter.

I do perceive the larger meaning in taking one obedient step at a time, that my own obedience to the Lord is the invitation for others to come to the table. As I write this last letter and pray into the dream, I feel I'm getting glimpses into a much bigger assignment.

It's not lost on me that a table represents a place where we gather as a family, where we pray, where we write. In the natural, I set our table today, flower vases and gold flatware included, for your send-off dinner. In a poignant way, I *felt* all the years captured in one moment of setting the table for all your special occasions and the beautiful ordinary days in between. It is my joy to set the table for those I dearly love.

Until we meet again at our kitchen table, we are close in heart.

I love you, Maddie.

Momma

Let not mercy and truth forsake thee:
bind them about thy neck;
write them upon the table of your heart.
(Proverbs 3:3 KJV)

P.S. I hope somewhere in Sweden you will find a "three-spline" fork for your dear old dad's table.

# Bonus Letter

## For My Readers

All around us God is writing a grand story of His love
and He invites us to let our lives fill the pages.
—Kristen McNulty, *Closed Doors*

Dear Readers,

Thank you for reading the words from my heart, addressed to my
precious daughter, but also for each of you. I hope my stories have
invited you to share your own.

May your heart perceive the larger messages of *27 Letters*.

If my words have stepped on your political or religious toes, please
pardon me. Your toes will heal.

If you're not already doing so, I hope you will begin the practice
of daily writing. Recording your life in writing will have a profound
effect toward a greater understanding of your divine purpose.

You will be amazed at the parallels, connected dots, confirmations, and synergy of your life as you record its unfolding in real time.

God is always trying to get your attention. And keep it.

Look up!
Write it down!

Cheers to you and your unique, beautiful story.

XoXo,

Angie

P.S. God loves you.

# About the Author

Angie goes to the grocery store in just her underwear.

Kidding aside, she has put her introverted self out on the farthest limb by inviting you into her personal journal.

Her writing is meant to be a graceful invitation to the inside of her conversations with God.

With pen in hand, heart on sleeve, and spirit on fire, she shares snapshots in time of her journey through a wilderness that only God can lead her through.

As a young child who moved often, she became fascinated with being a pen pal, consistently writing twenty-five letters a month for many years. She loved pens, stationery, and beautiful handwriting.

She currently resides with her family in a quaint little Pacific Northwest beach town. She enjoys baking, decorating and interior design, delicious pots of soup, good coffee, treasure hunting for vintage Christmas ornaments, and heart-to-heart conversations, especially with her daughters.

Her second book is unfolding via the same journal-style of weaving the stories of her life into the lives of those she loves. If you'd like to reach out to her, please write to her at FullCircleCoffeeCo510 @gmail.com.

Made in United States
Troutdale, OR
05/06/2024